ANTIQUITIES OF OLD RATHDOWN

Antiquities of Old Rathdown

Christiaan Corlett

First published in 1999
Wordwell Ltd
PO Box 69, Bray, Co. Wicklow
Copyright © Wordwell 1999.

Cover design: Nick Maxwell/Rachel Dunne

ISBN 1 869857 29 1

British Library Cataloguing-in-Publication Data.
A catalogue record for this book is available from the British Library.

This publication has received support from the Heritage Council under the 1999 Publications Grant Scheme.

Typeset in Ireland by Wordwell Ltd.

Book design: Nick Maxwell.

Origination by Wordwell Ltd.

Printed by Brookfield Printing Company.

All photographs © Chris Corlett except where otherwise indicated.

Contents

List of plates

List of figures

Acknowledgements

I would like to take this opportunity to thank the many people who were supportive of my work over the years and helped me to see this book through to publication. I am particularly indebted to Geraldine Stout of the Archaeological Survey of Ireland, *Dúchas* The Heritage Service, who provided the initial encouragement to carry out this work, and to Alison Bray and my family who were required to maintain that encouragement subsequently. Many thanks also to David Sweetman, Con Manning and Victor Buckley of the National Monuments Service, the Stone Axe Project, Leo Swan, James Eogan, John O'Neill, Malachy Conway, Rob Lynch and Dr Elizabeth O'Brien for their useful advice and information. Thanks also to Gwyn Bennett, Seán Downes and Karl Brady for their help in the field, and to John Scarry, Catherine Geraghty, Martin Bernon and Andrew Bonar Law for providing illustrations. Last, and by no means least, thanks are due to the staff of the Library of the Royal Society of Antiquaries of Ireland, the National Library of Ireland, the Irish Architectural Archive and the National Museum of Ireland. I would also like to express appreciation to my editor at Wordwell, Emer Condit, for her keen eye, suggestions and quest for perfection.

Foreword

I first met Chris Corlett when he was the auditor of the UCD Archaeological Society in 1993. I was impressed by his clear grasp of Irish archaeology and his enthusiasm for the subject. Since then Chris has spent much of his time working with us in *Dúchas,* and in particular with the Archaeological Survey. To the Survey he has brought his enthusiasm and keen understanding of our archaeological heritage. His experience on the Survey in Mayo, Roscommon and Longford clearly shows in this book.

This work is not merely an inventory or simple survey: it demonstrates a much broader sense of the total landscape and the background to the antiquities of the area which he describes so vividly. It is written in a straightforward style without academic jargon, and this is its strong point. South County Dublin and north Wicklow are the stamping-grounds of Chris Corlett, and his familiarity with the landscape and its antiquities is clearly reflected in his writing. The work is academically very sound, yet anyone with an interest in our heritage, monuments and antiquities will derive great pleasure from this book, even by dipping in and out of it or simply by using its most useful guide to the monuments.

David Sweetman
Chief Archaeologist
Dúchas

For my parents and Oma

Frontispiece—Oldcourt high cross base and tower-house.

Introduction

The Barony of Rathdown nestles between the fringes of the Wicklow and Dublin mountains to the west and the Irish Sea to the east. It stretches as far north as the city limits of Dublin, from Rathfarnham to Blackrock, and south to Delgany and Greystones in County Wicklow. In 1609 Rathdown Barony was divided in two by the establishment of the county boundary between Dublin and Wicklow. This border is essentially a modern one, and has been disregarded in this study.

This portrait of the archaeology of Rathdown is very much inspired by the aims of recent publications, in particular *Illustrated Irish archaeology*, edited by Michael Ryan (1991), and more recently *Ancient Ireland* by Jacqueline O'Brien and Peter Harbison (1996). Both books attempted to make archaeology accessible to a wider audience. The work presented here is a similar, but local, attempt to condense the wealth of information provided by previous researchers and, through the careful selection of illustrations, to make the archaeology of south-east Dublin and north-east Wicklow more accessible and understandable. Indeed, this book is dedicated to the many earlier scholars and their enormous contribution to the research of the archaeology of Rathdown.

Pl. 1—Ballybrack tomb.

SACRED SCULPTURE

South-east Dublin/north-east Wicklow is one of the fastest-developing areas in Ireland, with new factories and houses springing up at an incredible rate. Today the dolmen at Ballybrack near Shankill appears more like a modern sculpture in a residential estate than a sacred tomb built over 5000 years ago. In the face of such threats it is all the more important that we celebrate our unique archaeological surroundings in order to preserve them for the speculations of future generations. In the meantime, let us admire and wonder at these monuments from and to the past, for they are our only physical links with our ancestors.

While much of the information in this book is borrowed, this is the first attempt at an archaeological synthesis of south-east Dublin and north-east Wicklow. Also, for the first time this book will consider the stray finds from this area, which have previously been ignored. The book attempts to be both general and comprehensive, and I hope that the reader will be able to browse through the general archaeology of Rathdown as well as focus on specific sites or themes. All too often the grass is greener on the other side and we overlook that which surrounds us. In this book I wish to celebrate the rich archaeological and historical heritage that survives almost literally in our back gardens. This is more important than ever in the light of the increasing dangers to that fragile heritage posed by urban development, which threatens to spread its houses, roads and industries across many archaeological sites, many of which have until now survived unmolested for thousands of years. The archaeological resource is frequently undervalued, and if this book is to achieve anything I hope it illustrates how special and precious that resource is. Surely no price is too high to preserve these sites, these monuments to our ancestors.

The physical landscape

Rathdown is perhaps best known for the scenic beauty and splendour of its mountains, river valleys and coastline. The basic geological ingredients of this complex landscape consist of quartzites, shale and sandstones at Bray Head, the quartzite peaks of the Great and Little Sugar Loafs, and the granite of the Wicklow Mountains as well as at Dalkey and Blackrock, which formed millions of years ago when the island of Ireland did not exist as we know it today. Water has enhanced the visual delight of these basic ingredients in various ways, in particular in its most voracious form, ice, which developed after the cooling of the climate some two million years ago.

The Ice Age spawned glaciers in the mountains, forming corry lakes with their steep-sided cliffs, such as Upper and Lower Lough Bray. Despite brief periods of respite, these great sheets of ice crept across the uplands and

Pl. 2—Bray Head.

'A SLEEPING WHALE'

'. . . the blunt cape of Bray Head that lay on the water like the snout of a sleeping whale' (James Joyce, *Ulysses*).

The quartzite, shale and sandstone rocks of Bray Head were formed over 500 million years ago, and are among the oldest rocks in the area. They are an important source of fossils, recording ancient life-forms.

AN ICY MEMORY

The snow-capped Dublin and Wicklow mountains provide a reminder of a land covered in ice for thousands of years, before the ice-sheets finally retreated only 10,000 years ago.

Pl. 3—The Wicklow Mountains in the snow.

lowlands, rounding off the peaks of the Wicklow Mountains, sculpting many valleys, such as Glencree, and dumping the off-cuts as they went. A massive sheet of ice developed in the area formerly (and later) occupied by the Irish Sea, extending as far inland as the foothills of the mountains. This ice transported and then dumped on the mainland huge quantities of clay containing marine shells scoured from the bed of the sea. These clays are today clearly visible along the coast from Killiney to Greystones, and contain limestone boulders that are otherwise not native to the area.

Towards the end of the Ice Age melted water formed enormous lakes, such as the one in the area of Fassaroe and Enniskerry. The sand and gravel deposited at the bottoms of these lakes formed a delta, and have been useful for quarrying in more recent times. The waters of this lake built up, being trapped by the mountains to the west and the ice-sheets to the east in the Irish Sea. Eventually, the pressures created by the incredible volume of water found a weakness in the underlying bedrock and gouged out massive, steep valleys at

'A LOFTY MASS OF IMPENDING ROCKS'

The antiquarian Austin Cooper, who visited the Scalp in 1781, wrote: 'On each side as you pass you are overawed by a lofty Mass of impending Rocks, threatening destruction at every instant — some projecting & cracked as if ready to fall — others already fallen in monstrous pieces, & strewed on each side of the road.' Cooper was convinced that the valley was created by 'the Effect of some internal Commotion in the Bowels of the Earth'. The artist Gabriel Beranger in 1779 thought that the Scalp was 'a mountain split in two by some earthquake, or other revolution, time out of mind', and that the enormous rocks 'seem ready to tumble down and crush the amazed traveller'. Today we know that the valley was carved out by the raging waters of the melting ice over 12,000 years ago.

Pl. 4—The Scalp.

the Rocky Valley, the Scalp and the Glen of the Downs. Today their tiny streams are a slight testimony to the great flood-waters that created them.

About 11,000 years ago the ice gradually began to melt, and wildlife began to colonise from western Europe. Juniper, willow and birch took hold; giant deer and reindeer wandered the scrubland at the edges of the forests, and sought water at the shores of lakes such as Ballybetagh near Kiltiernan. The lake here was drained and reclaimed in more recent times, and the enormous

THE ICE-SHEETS RETREAT

About 10,000 years ago the climate finally improved and forced the great ice-sheets into retreat.

Pl. 5—Sunset over the Wicklow and Dublin mountains.

antlers of the giant Irish elk were found there in large quantities. For about 500 years the ice returned, but the elk did not. When the ice-sheets finally retreated northwards about 10,000 years ago, hazel and pine woodlands developed, followed by oak, elm, alder and ash. By the time the first human settlers came to Ireland, about 9000 years ago, they found an island covered in deep forests, which soon became dominated by hazel and oak. In upland areas, such as the Wicklow Mountains, pine forests thrived, as evidenced by the stumps found beneath the blanket bog which now covers these slopes. This bog, which today typifies the high slopes of the mountains, began to develop about 4000 years ago, largely owing to climatic deterioration and human interference.

Today, human intervention is more obvious in south-east Dublin and north-east Wicklow. The relentless waves of urban sprawl throughout so much of this area illustrate the human desire to control the landscape. However, this is not a new phenomenon: the human impact on the landscape has been gradual but effective. Archaeology can trace the human desire both to understand and to control nature since the first settlers arrived on these shores over 9000 years ago.

The overwhelming beauty of the landscape of south-east Dublin and north-east Wicklow has, not surprisingly, overshadowed the human heritage of the area. George Bernard Shaw, who lived for a time at Dalkey, was so inspired by his surroundings that he wrote: 'I lived on a hill top with the most beautiful view in the world—I had only to open my eyes to see such pictures as no painter could make for me'. While we are lucky to have inherited this natural beauty, we often overlook the thousands of years of human influence which have also shaped this landscape. Our archaeological heritage is a testimony to the achievements of our ancestors.

Pl. 6—Sunset behind the Great Sugar Loaf, seen from Coolagad.

'A GENTLEMANLY MOUNTAIN'

'Behold that mountain tow'ring, rugged, high,

That culminating, daring, braves the sky:

Planted on broad and solid rocky base,

Impregnable in strength assumes its place'

—extract from a poem by Isaac Corry, allegedly written in the parlour of Henry Grattan at Tinnehinch, near Enniskerry. Thomas Cromwell, in his travel guide of Leinster published in 1820, wrote that the mountain seemed 'to look in pride upon the comparatively diminutive subjects around it'. Eugene O'Curry, of the Ordnance Survey, climbed the Sugar Loaf in December 1838, and afterwards wrote: 'though anxious I may be for elevation in this world, I hope never again will have occasion to rise so high in it'.

Canon Scott in 1913 described the Great Sugar Loaf in more personal terms: 'Look at him over there! Isn't he a gentlemanly mountain? From whatever point of view you look at him, he always looks a fine gentleman — just a trifle aloof from the rest, as if he could not help feeling his superiority, but benevolent and friendly all the same, and never can you catch him in a clumsy or vulgar attitude.'

The Stone Age

THE EARLIEST HUMAN SETTLERS

In terms of human settlement, despite popular belief, Ireland is very young. People had been living in southern Britain and other parts of Europe from about 250,000 years ago, and by the time man first arrived in Ireland all the continents of the world, including the Americas (inaccurately known as the New World) and Australia, had been colonised. The ice-sheets that covered much of Ireland for nearly two million years seem to have deterred settlers from advancing as far as this country, despite the fact that the sea-levels may have been low enough to allow a person to walk from France to Britain and across to Ireland. The last great ice-sheets finally left Ireland's shores about 10,000 years ago, and gradually woodlands expanded and began to dominate the Irish landscape. The first human pioneers reached Ireland some time before 7000 BC. Perhaps it is typically Irish that the story of human settlement

Pl. 7—Woodlands of the Dargle Valley.

THE DARGLE VALLEY

The first settlers arrived in a densely wooded landscape consisting mainly of hazel scrub, which was later replaced by tall canopy forest such as oak, pine, elm and ash. River valleys, such as the Dargle Valley, formed natural routeways inland through these forests, and the hazel and oak woodlands here are typical of the landscape in which the early hunters roamed before the introduction of farming. In a letter to his wife in 1825, John Gibson Lockhart wrote: 'The Dargle, superior even to its name—an indiscriminately beautiful mixture of wood, water, rocks, hills, valley'.

DALKEY ISLAND

Excavations on Dalkey Island revealed large collections of sea shells mixed with flint tools (known as Bann Flakes) typically used by our ancestors nearly 6000 years ago. There were also the bones of a variety of other sea creatures, including dolphin, conger eel, wrasse, mullet, cod and tope. The presence of dolphin and tope, normally found in deeper waters, suggests that the islanders had seaworthy vessels. Also found were the bones of a variety of birds, including the white-tailed sea eagle, goshawk, razorbill/guillemot and puffin. Bones of seal and brown bear provide evidence for hunting, and clearly the bear would have been hunted on the mainland. It appears that these people were not simply paying short visits to the island, but were living there for long periods of time.

Pl. 8—Sunrise at Dalkey Island.

in this country should start in the middle—that is, the Middle Stone Age or Mesolithic period.

The earliest people to arrive on these shores were hunters, fishers and gatherers who used a stone technology. They may have first settled in the north-east of Ireland, an area rich in flint, which was the best material available with which to make stone tools. Over the next 3500 years their hunting and fishing life-style changed little, despite dramatic changes in the landscape during this time. Sea-levels rose and fell, hazel scrub was replaced by tall canopy forest such as oak, pine, elm and ash, and in the Irish midlands many of the smaller lakes became choked up and were transformed into raised bogs. The diverse Irish

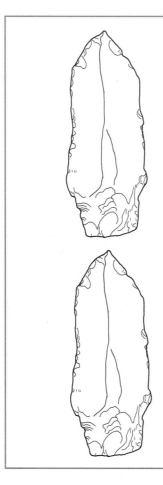

Fig. 1—Bann Flakes from Rathfarnham (courtesy of the National Museum of Ireland ©).

EVIDENCE OF THE EARLIEST SETTLERS

These typical Bann Flakes from Rathfarnham are trimmed along the long edges and at one end to provide a primitive point. Such crude implements were probably used as projectile points for hunting and fishing, or as knives for use in food preparation and other domestic chores. Many would originally have been hafted in a wooden handle. These tools are often the only evidence of the earliest settlers. The temporary houses of these nomadic hunters and fishers have long since disappeared, and they do not seem to have constructed religious monuments. Perhaps their temples were the very forests, rivers and mountains that surrounded them.

landscape provided a mixed diet, including wild pig, red deer, salmon, trout, eels, sea fish, shellfish, and woodland and coastal birds, as well as the fruits of the forest. The earliest settlers built only temporary dwellings—small, domed huts of timber stakes, covered in deer hides or turves of sod. They were nomadic people, never staying long in one place and always in search of the next meal. They would take all their possessions with them, including their deer hides, which could be used again in the construction of a new house.

The current archaeological evidence suggests that south-east Dublin was first inhabited at the end of the Mesolithic period (5000–3300 BC). At this time people made crude flint tools known as 'Bann Flakes', so called because they were first recognised by archaeologists in large numbers on the River Bann. Flint, though very hard, can be easily worked by chipping to create a razor-sharp edge, suitable for a wide range of domestic and hunting implements. Stones such as quartz and chert, among others, were also useful. Small numbers of Bann Flakes have been found at Dalkey Island, Dun Laoghaire, Rathfarnham and Loughlinstown, indicating small-scale settlement along rivers, streams and the coast. Coastal areas from Killiney to Bray and north of Greystones, which had important resources of flint pebbles as well as food, are subject to extensive erosion, and any evidence for early occupation along these shores has probably been long since washed away by the rough seas. However, important evidence has survived on Dalkey Island, where Bann Flakes were found in large collections or middens of sea shells, radiocarbon-dated to about 3340 BC. A selection of fish, bird and other animal bones were also found, illustrating the diverse diet of the islanders.

THE BEGINNINGS OF AGRICULTURE

Between 10,000 and 8000 BC the practice of farming was developed in the Middle East, in an area known as the 'Fertile Crescent', stretching from the River Nile to the River Tigris. Farming gradually spread across Europe, and was introduced into Ireland shortly after 4000 BC, bringing many radical changes

Pl. 9—
Brennanstown
portal tomb.

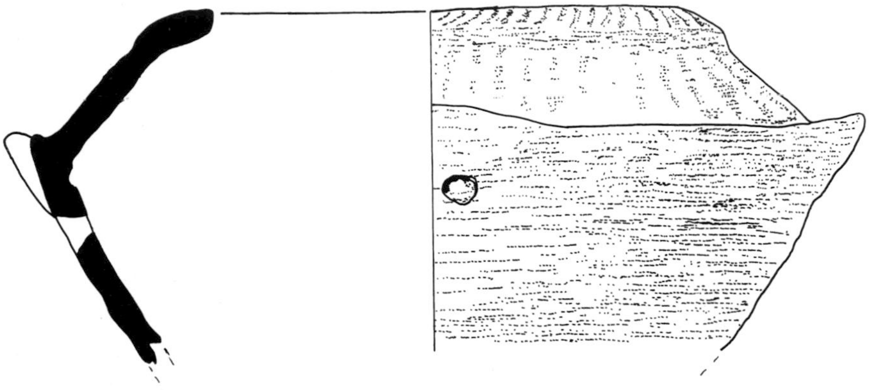

Fig. 2—Neolithic pottery from Dalkey Island (after Liversage 1968).

THE FIRST FARMERS

This little pot from Dalkey Island is among the earliest pottery vessels in Ireland, which were manufactured by the first farmers. They were hand-made from rings or coils of clay and then baked at temperatures of around 800˚C in above-ground fires or within firing-pits. The pots were often decorated all over the outer surface with cord or shell impressions, or by a technique known as stab-and-drag, in which a pointed or flat-tipped piece of bone or stick was drawn across the wet pottery before it was baked. They could be used for domestic purposes, but were also used as grave-goods in megalithic tombs.

which affected all aspects of life. Farmers now attempted to control their food supply, with the aim of providing a surplus for leaner times of the year. In order to domesticate and maintain animals and plants it was necessary to open up the landscape by removing areas of woodland and creating fields. For a time forests continued to dominate the countryside, and contained hidden dangers such as bears, wolves and wild boars. Domesticated dogs provided useful protection.

The cultivation of cereals and the maintenance of stock required people to settle down within an area and to construct more permanent houses. New technology evolved to facilitate this new economy and way of life, including stone axes to remove the trees and pottery to store food. Querns for grinding cereals were developed, and are often called 'saddle querns' because of the shape they acquired after constant use. Two saddle querns were recently found to the north of Tully church in Lehaunstown, during excavations by Edmond O'Donovan.

Pl. 10—A magnificent flint javelin-head (6.6cm long) found during excavations on Dalkey Island (courtesy of the National Museum of Ireland ©).

As people put down roots, changes in social organisation took place. The division of the year became essential in order to establish sowing and harvesting seasons. The early farmers built enormous stone tombs as monuments to the dead, and new religions developed, revolving around new gods or deities directly associated with the new economy and the new landscape. In Ireland the change to farming was probably slow, but nonetheless dramatic. Indeed, these changes were some of the most dramatic to occur at any time in Irish prehistory, and the dominance of agriculture today in the Irish economy is a tribute to those pioneer farmers who arrived on this island nearly 6000 years ago. Perhaps their importance is highlighted by the fact that the basic economic ingredients of farming—cereals, cattle, sheep and goat—were not native to Ireland, and had to be brought into the country at this time. However, the farming way of life did not replace the earlier hunting and fishing life-style all at once. Among the collections of waste sea shells left behind by the hunters and fishers living on Dalkey Island, sherds of pottery and the bones of domesticated cattle were also found. It appears that for a few hundred years people who survived by hunting and fishing in the forests, rivers and seas lived side by side with the first farmers as they cleared their fields, harvested their first crops, and tended the first generations of cattle and sheep born on Irish soil.

NEW STONE TOOLS

The end of the Stone Age is known as the Neolithic or New Stone Age, a term used to describe the new stone technology brought by the early farmers. In Ireland this new technology is represented by a range of stone arrowheads, scrapers, knives and axeheads, as well as by the use of pottery. Flint and chert were the principal materials used to create most tools. Unique to Ireland are hollow scrapers, with their distinctive C-shaped scraping edge, perhaps designed for the preparation of arrow-shafts or for reaping. Several such hollow scrapers have been found at Kiltiernan portal tomb. The manufacture of arrowheads, typically leaf- or lozenge-shaped, indicates that hunting still made an important contribution to the food supply, or that warfare had developed in Irish society. Several examples of arrowheads were found during excavations at Kiltiernan portal tomb, Taylor's Grange portal tomb, and on Dalkey Island. Further arrowheads have been recovered as stray finds, for example at Carrickmines, Rathfarnham and Whitechurch.

Polished stone axeheads are typical of this period, and are commonly found in the area. Their manufacture involved a long and complex process. First the stone was flaked into a rough-out, and was then polished or ground down by rubbing on a wetted sandstone. The final polish may have been produced by burnishing with a soft leather cloth; its polished edges made the implement less susceptible to breakage. However, before the process could begin, the raw material had to be obtained, and very often local stone was not chosen. The

Pl. 11—Flint scrapers and a chert arrowhead from Kiltiernan portal tomb (courtesy of the National Museum of Ireland ©).

STATUS SYMBOLS?

Stone axes vary in size and shape. Some examples, such as those found at Dun Laoghaire and Dundrum, are waisted, with a wide but shallow groove towards the butt end to help secure the axehead within its timber handle. Experiments have demonstrated that stone axes could be used successfully for felling trees. Other types, such as an example from Kilmacanogue which is shaped more like an adze, may have been intended for more specific carpentry needs. However, the fact that many of these axes are made of porcellanite, a stone which had to be brought to the area from over 100 miles away to the north, suggests that they were seen as more than just implements for felling trees. It is clear that many served as status symbols and recent research indicates that they may have played important ceremonial roles.

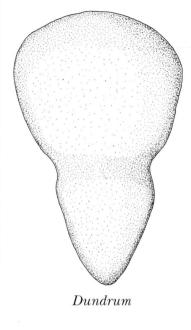

Dundrum

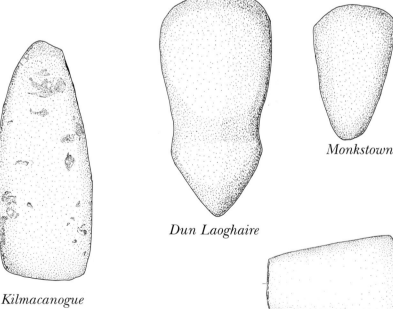

Kilmacanogue

Dun Laoghaire

Monkstown

Blackrock

Fig. 3—Stone axes from Blackrock, Dundrum, Dun Laoghaire, Kilmacanogue and Monkstown (reproduced at two-thirds scale). (Courtesy of the National Museum of Ireland ©.)

'A SPHINX-LIKE MONSTER'

The portal tomb at Kiltiernan was poetically described by Borlase in 1897 as 'a sphinx-like monster, advancing out of the rocky hill on some half-dozen short and rickety legs'. The giant capstone is estimated to weigh over 25 tonnes. How the earliest farmers, using only stone technology, managed to lift it onto the supporting stones remains a mystery.

Pl. 12—Kiltiernan portal tomb.

most popular stone used in the manufacture of these axes was porcellanite, the only sources of which can be found at Tievebulliagh Mountain and on Rathlin Island, both in County Antrim. Axes made of porcellanite have been found at Blackrock, Three Rock Mountain (Ballyedmonduff) and Dun Laoghaire. A stone axe found at Murphystown is made from porphyry, and recently Dr Gabriel Cooney of the Stone Axe Project discovered the 5000-year-old mining sites for porphyry on Lambay Island, off Skerries in north County Dublin.

MEGALITHIC TOMBS

The first farmers also engineered and constructed impressive religious monuments known as megalithic tombs, a Greek term which refers to the large stones employed in their construction. Megalithic tombs were the first permanent structures built in Ireland and are an important reflection of the attempts made by the first farmers to organise the landscape around them. They not only served as tributes to those buried within, but were probably also used as ceremonial centres for the people who built and lived near them. These tombs also highlight the divisions within society, as they were probably constructed to contain and mark the burials of the community leaders rather than of the actual builders.

Several different forms of megalithic tomb were built in Ireland. The most common type in Rathdown are known as portal tombs because of the characteristic portal stones which form their entrance. These portal or entrance stones support a dramatic roof stone, which often rests on a smaller

Pl. 13—Glensouthwell portal tomb.

THE DRUID'S CHAIR

The remains of a portal tomb, known locally as the Brehon's or Druid's Chair, at Glensouthwell, Taylor's Grange. In 1776 the antiquarian artist Gabriel Beranger wrote: 'it is supposed to have been a Seat of Judgement for the Arch Druid, or a place from where he delivered his oracles, it has the form of an Easy Chair wanting only the seat'.

Pl. 14—Dolmen at Ballybrack, near Shankill.

stone at the rear of the tomb. The term 'dolmen', also used to describe these monuments, derives from the Breton *daul* (table) and *maen* (stone). Edmond O'Donovan recently noticed that in several instances a door stone, set between the two portal stones, does not serve any practical structural function other than to block the entrance into the tomb. This implies that access to the burial chamber was intended to be restricted, and perhaps these tombs were not originally meant to be used for further burials after their construction. That is not to say that later generations complied with this intention, and the tombs probably continued to serve as ceremonial and burial monuments.

Some of the most monumental tombs ever built anywhere in the world are the passage tombs in the Boyne Valley, such as Newgrange, Knowth and Dowth. These tombs take their name from the stone passage that provides access to a burial chamber within a large, circular, earth and stone mound. An important series of passage tombs stretches across the south Dublin and west Wicklow mountains, and the easternmost example occurs on the summit of Two Rock Mountain. The site of the tomb was well chosen, and Killiney Head, Bray Head and the Great Sugar Loaf are visible to the east and south-east. However, the most spectacular view from the tomb is northwards, overlooking the city of Dublin, from Tallaght to Howth. Even until relatively recently much of this area we now know as Dublin City was primarily rural agricultural land, and farmers working their fields 5000 years ago would have been familiar with the tomb, which appears as a small lump on the head of Two Rock Mountain. They might have been able to tell us the names of the people buried there, and may even have visited the site to pay their respects.

'LEABA NA SAIGHE'

This 1851 drawing by Henry O'Neill is all that survives of a dolmen known as *Leaba na Saighe*, the 'hound's bed or grave', at Ballybrack near Glencullen, destroyed about 1860.

Fig. 4—Destroyed dolmen at Ballybrack, near Glencullen.

The Early Bronze Age

THE BEGINNINGS OF METAL-WORKING

Pl. 15—Cairns on the northern shoulder of the Great Sugar Loaf.

The idea of producing objects from metal ores, initially copper, arrived in Ireland nearly 4500 years ago, at a time when the Egyptian and Mesopotamian civilisations of the Near East were flourishing. These people had already begun to document their history and had mastered metal technology when Ireland and the rest of Europe continued to trek through the depths of the Stone Age. Copper ores can be found in several places throughout Ireland, and the earliest people to use this technology extracted their ores from copper mines such as that at Ross Island, near Killarney in County Kerry. The copper ore was then smelted at the required heat of 1200°C to produce copper cakes which could be more easily transported around the country. Two fragments of copper cake and three damaged copper axes, probably intended to be recycled, were found at Monastery, near Enniskerry. These copper cakes were ingots which could be

HUNTING GROUNDS

The quartz barbed and tanged arrowhead (Fig. 5) from Powerscourt Mountain was found on the ridge between Lough Bray Upper and Lower. Another barbed and tanged arrowhead of flint was found in a pass up the cliff face above the cold, deep waters of Lough Bray Lower, a lake-filled glacial corry high in the Wicklow Mountains. Perhaps it was lost by a hunter on the mountains over 4000 years ago, lying in wait for deer using this pass.

Despite the development of metal production, stone continued to be used to   make many utensils, in particular tiny barbed and tanged arrowheads, such as this flint example found in the vicinity of Dundrum and Ballinteer, and a quartz example from Powerscourt Mountain, the latter only 2.5cm long and 2cm wide. These are highly accomplished pieces, and their entire surface has been carefully shaped and worked.

Pl. 16—Lough Bray Lower.

Fig. 5—Barbed and tanged arrowheads from Dundrum/ Ballinteer and Powerscourt Mountain.

melted down and then poured into a stone mould bearing a carved impression of the finished product, such as daggers or axes. Flat copper axes were the most common products manufactured with this new technology, and have been found at Bray, Dalkey, Dalkey Island, Cabinteely, Carmanhall, Glencullen, Killincarrig and Newtown. These early experimenters with copper also produced daggers, such as an example (now lost) from Glencullen Mountain.

Over time these metal-workers learned to mix tin with copper to produce bronze, which formed a more rigid blade. Advances in casting which allowed for the manufacture of a more durable product are reflected in attempts to improve the hafting of axes. The flat copper axes, the earliest in the series, were primitively hafted through a timber handle and strapped into place. However, this method of hafting was not very secure, and as casting methods improved so too did the design of the axe. The new designs concentrated on improving the butt end, where these implements were hafted, resulting in the development of the palstave, which was cast in a two-piece mould. The palstave had the added

VALUABLE TOOLS

The earliest copper axes, such as these from Bray and Cabinteely, were probably expensive to produce; they could not be afforded by everyone in society and became a valuable form of currency. The example from Bray, decorated with lightly incised ornament, may not have been simply a tool for cutting wood, and was perhaps used as a symbol of its owner's wealth.

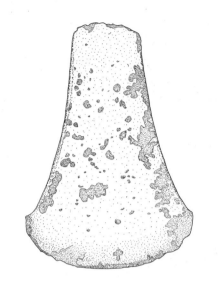

Fig. 6—Flat axes from Bray and Cabinteely (courtesy of the National Museum of Ireland ©).

5 cm.

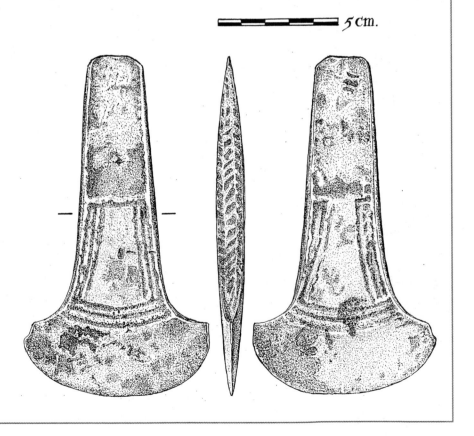

WEAPONS

Fig. 7—Palstave from Bray.
This palstave was found in a pool in the Dargle River near Bray. Was it simply lost by its owner nearly 4000 years ago, or was it deliberately thrown into the river as a sacrifice to a river god?

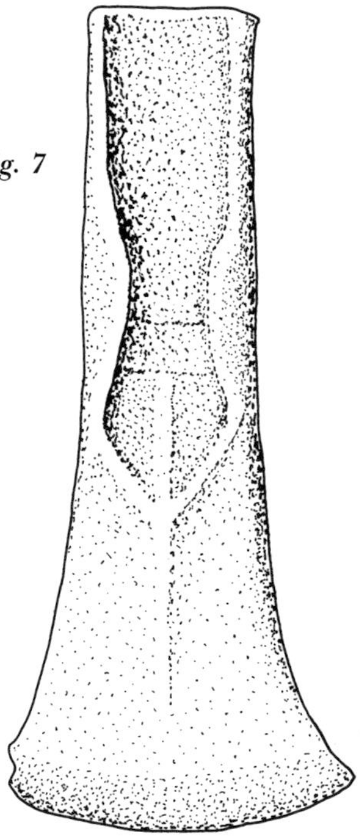

Fig. 7

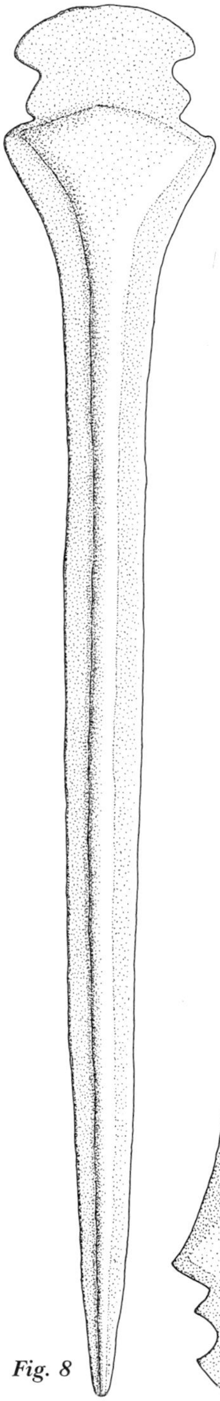

Fig. 8—Rapier from Mount Mepas.
A fine rapier from Mount Mepas on Killiney Hill with a narrow blade, 26cm long and only 4mm thick.

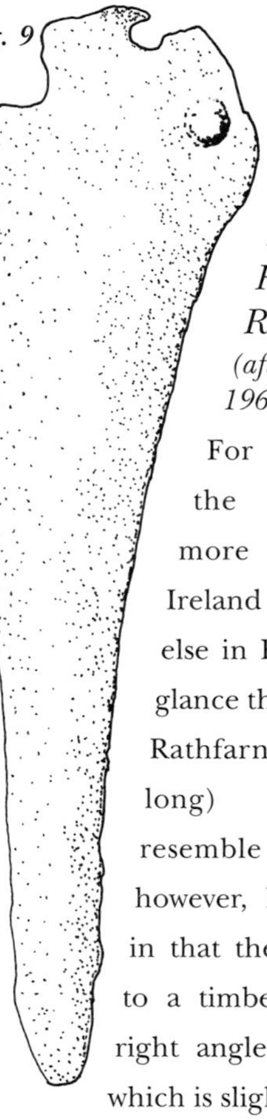

Fig. 8

Fig. 10

Fig. 9

*Fig. 9—
Halberd from
Rathfarnham
(after Harbison
1969).*

For some reason the halberd was more popular in Ireland than anywhere else in Europe. At first glance the halberd from Rathfarnham (26.6cm long) appears to resemble a dagger; however, halberds differ in that they were riveted to a timber handle at a right angle to the blade, which is slightly curved and blunt. They seem to have been designed as a weapon for striking an enemy, rather than piercing like a dagger.

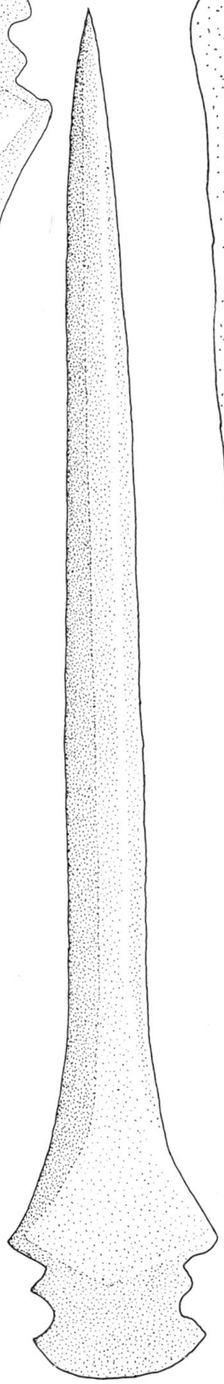

Fig. 10—Bronze rapier from Featherbed Mountain.
This fine bronze rapier, 26.7cm long, was found in 1941 by a turf-cutter working on the bog at Featherbed Mountain, near Glencree.

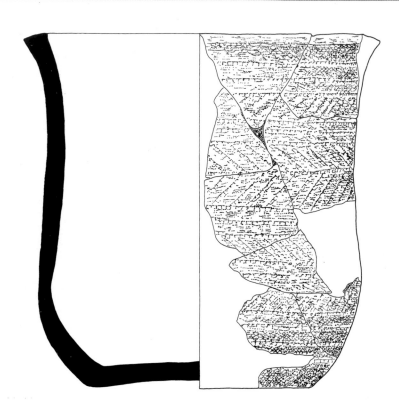

Fig. 11—Beaker pot from Dalkey Island (after Liversage 1968).

BEAKER POTTERY

The earliest metal-workers throughout much of Europe are often associated with a distinctive type of pottery known as Beaker pottery. These elegant pots are frequently decorated all over with a variety of patterns. As the name implies, they may have been used for the consumption of beverages. Beakers have been recovered from archaeological excavations at tombs such as Ballyedmonduff wedge tomb and settlement sites such as Dalkey Island, and more recently by James Eogan at Rathdown Lower.

benefit of flanges along the edges and a stop ridge at the base of the blade, which provided for a more secure hafting. Such palstaves have been found at Belmont Demesne, Bray and Glenamuck. However, as might be expected, these early metal-workers were not infallible. The palstave from Belmont Demesne was carelessly made, because the two halves of the mould were incorrectly aligned when the artefact was being manufactured. The fine copper rapier from Mount Mepas on Killiney Hill and the halberd from Rathfarnham were also made using two-piece stone moulds.

BURIAL TRADITIONS

At the beginning of the Bronze Age megalithic tombs known as wedge tombs, such as at Ballyedmonduff, were constructed, indicating that the megalithic tradition survived the new changes in technology. Often the entrances of these tombs face west, perhaps in the direction of the setting sun. From 2000 to 1600 BC burial rites became tremendously varied. Cremations and skeletons (sometimes disarticulated) were buried in a range of tombs, and were often accompanied by, or even contained within, a fascinating range of specially designed pottery types. Some burials were covered by stone cairns, for example on the northern shoulder of the Great Sugar Loaf, and by earthen mounds or

Pl. 17—Collared Urn, Encrusted Urn, Food Vessels and Pygmy Cup from Edmondstown (courtesy of the National Museum of Ireland ©).

VESSELS FOR THE DEAD

Often associated with Early Bronze Age burials is a range of funerary pottery, such as this selection from a cemetery at Edmondstown. The large vessels are cinerary urns, designed specifically to contain the cremated remains of one or more individuals, and they were often placed inverted within the grave. Encrusted Urns take their name from the encrusted ornamentation on their outer surface, while Collared Urns are named after a distinctive collar around their neck. The function of the tiny vessel, known as a Pygmy Cup, is uncertain, though it has sometimes been suggested that they contained incense. The bowl- and vase-shaped Food Vessels are often the only grave-good found with Early Bronze Age burials and are generally believed to have contained some form of food or beverage offering, perhaps intended to accompany the deceased on the journey into the afterlife.

A TYPICAL WEDGE TOMB

The tomb at Ballyedmonduff is typical of the wedge tombs built at the time of the first use of metal in Ireland, and is among the last megalithic tombs to be constructed in the country. It was excavated in 1945 by Seán P. Ó Ríordáin and Ruaidhrí de Valéra, and within the burial gallery were found sherds of four Beaker pots, a stone macehead, and a small amount of cremated human bone.

Pl. 18—Ballyedmonduff wedge tomb.

NEOLITHIC ROCK ART

Pl. 19—Rock art at Ballyedmonduff wedge tomb.

Lying loose on the southern side of the cairn of the Ballyedmonduff wedge tomb is a granite block, on one surface of which are seven cupmarks. Such cupmarks are associated with a form of decoration

on stone known as rock art, believed to be of Neolithic date. Such art is normally found on natural rock outcrop rather than on the stones of a tomb. Perhaps the decorated stone was broken off a natural boulder and brought to this site when the tomb was built at the beginning of the Bronze Age.

HUMAN SACRIFICE?

The cist found beside the obelisk at Stillorgan Park in 1955 contained the disturbed remains of the skeleton of an adult female, whose death was caused by a (sacrificial?) blow to the skull.

Pl. 20—Cist burial at Stillorgan (courtesy of the National Museum of Ireland ©).

tumuli on lower ground, such as at Monastery near Enniskerry. At Kilmashogue the wedge tomb was reused. Other burials were placed within stone-lined graves or in simple pits dug in the ground, sometimes forming cemeteries, such as at Edmondstown near Rathfarnham, and were apparently not marked by any sort of monument. Today such burials are usually found by chance, for example during gravel-quarrying or ploughing. Burials were found during the construction of Stillorgan House at the beginning of the eighteenth century.

Fig. 12— Ballybrew, Cist 1 (after Martin, Price and Mitchell 1935–7).

EARLY BRONZE AGE BURIAL

Early Bronze Age burials sometimes occur in unmarked cemeteries. This skeleton of a young adult female was placed in a crouched position in a small, rectangular, stone-lined

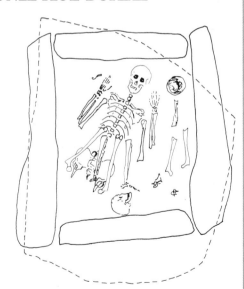

grave, in a small cemetery at Ballybrew. A Bowl Food Vessel, which appears to have been placed on a rush matting, stood opposite the face of the deceased.

The Later Bronze Age and Iron Age: the end of prehistory

Pl. 21—Newtown standing stone.

SOPHISTICATED TECHNOLOGY

By the end of the Bronze Age, from 1200 to 600 BC, metal-workers, in both gold and bronze, had become highly skilled and confident at their trade. The development of clay moulds allowed the manufacture of more sophisticated bronze pieces. During the excavations on Dalkey Island a large number of Late Bronze Age clay mould fragments were found, indicating an important metal-working production site, particularly of socketed axeheads and spearheads. The socketed form of axe allowed for very secure hafting. Such axes have been found at Killincarrig, Kindlestown, Rathfarnham, Stillorgan and Ticknock. This was a time of rising wealth, reflected by two gold personal ornaments found at Rathfarnham and Monkstown. A spearhead from Rathmichael near Shankill may reflect a new concern with weaponry in the light of rising wealth. It may be no coincidence that in Rathmichael the top of a hill was enclosed by a large

GOLD-WORKING

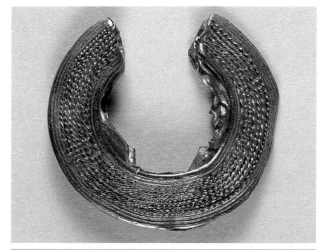

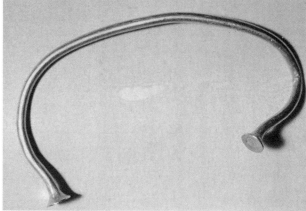

By 700 BC Irish gold-working had become highly developed and accomplished, producing some of the most spectacular gold artefacts from any period in Ireland. This is represented in south-east Dublin by a hair ornament called a lock-ring from Rathfarnham, and a penannular bracelet from near Monkstown. The gold bracelet was found bent out of shape. It consists of a round-sectioned gold wire (3mm in diameter, 8cm long), with trumpet-shaped terminals. The tiny gold lock-ring from Rathfarnham, unfortunately crushed flat over time, is only 1.9cm in diameter. Each face-plate consists of a central band of eight twisted wires (each only 1mm thick), bounded on the inside and outside by a band of three or four plain wires. It was found about 1860 by a man screening gravel taken out of the bed of the River Dodder. Also found in Rathfarnham, in 1855, though not illustrated here, was a small gold ribbed ring, which may originally have been threaded onto a bracelet similar to the one from Monkstown.

defensive rampart, forming a hillfort, which appears to represent the focus of some political centre in south-east Dublin around 1000 BC.

Pl. 22— Rathfarnham lock-ring and Monkstown penannular bracelet (courtesy of the National Museum of Ireland ©).

FULACHTA FIADH

Fulachta fiadh are mounds of burnt stone traditionally associated with the festivities of hunting parties of the Fianna cooking their kill of deer. Archaeological excavation has shown that these were most commonly used between 1500 and 1000 BC. Experiments have shown how fulachta fiadh were used: after being heated in a hot fire, the stones were placed into a rectangular stone or timber trough filled with water. The hot stones would then heat the water to boiling point, and the temperature could be maintained by adding hot

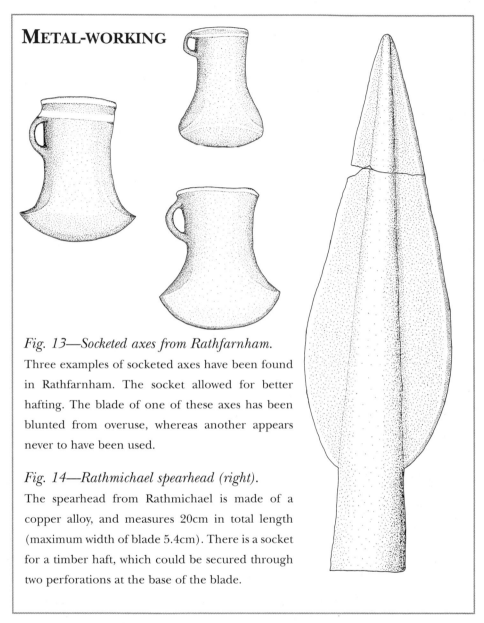

METAL-WORKING

Fig. 13—Socketed axes from Rathfarnham.
Three examples of socketed axes have been found in Rathfarnham. The socket allowed for better hafting. The blade of one of these axes has been blunted from overuse, whereas another appears never to have been used.

Fig. 14—Rathmichael spearhead (right).
The spearhead from Rathmichael is made of a copper alloy, and measures 20cm in total length (maximum width of blade 5.4cm). There is a socket for a timber haft, which could be secured through two perforations at the base of the blade.

stones from the fire every so often. Averaging 20 minutes to the pound for meat, this was not altogether a primitive method of cooking, but it was time-consuming and may have been reserved for special occasions. However, there are several problems with the idea that these burnt mounds were associated with cooking, primarily the lack of evidence for food remains at excavated sites. Therefore other functions have been proposed, such as ceremonial bathing, or that the hot water produced was intended for some kind of industrial use, such as textile crafts. Examples have been excavated at Ballyremon Commons Killincarrig, and most recently at Shankill.

THE AGE OF IRON

Archaeologists traditionally consider the Bronze Age to end sometime after 600 BC, heralding the beginning of a new period known as the Iron Age, which continued to about AD 400, when Christianity was introduced into Ireland. This is a period which saw the rise and fall of many great Mediterranean civilisations, such as the Etruscans, the Greeks and the mighty Roman Empire. The old Celtic Irish epics recall a heroic age of kings and warriors, a time of conflict between Medb, the warrior queen of Connacht, and Conor Mac Nessa, king of Ulster and protector of the legendary warrior Cú Chulainn. However, if the Celts ever arrived in Rathdown they left no obvious evidence for the archaeologist, casting a silent shadow of mystery over the centuries before and after the birth of Christ. No artefacts dating from this period have been found in south-east Dublin or north-east Wicklow, and several of the monuments in this area, such as standing stones and hillforts, could date from either the Late Bronze Age or the Iron Age.

Pl. 23—Kilmashogue standing stone.

STANDING STONES

The function of standing stones remains a mystery, though there can be no doubt that their apparent simplicity masks a whole range of rituals and ceremonies carried out at these sites. Some standing stones appear to have marked burials (not unlike modern headstones), and excavations by Judith Carroll of the soil immediately around a standing stone at Cabinteely produced two fragments of cremated human bone. Others may have been territorial markers, or perhaps recorded places where important events occurred. The dating of standing stones is also problematic, and while some may date from the Celtic Iron Age, many appear to be earlier.

'QUEEN MAB'

In Glencullen is a large quartz standing stone, 1.83m high, known locally as 'Queen Mab'. Apparently there was another similar stone near the old church in the village, and in 1837 Eugene O'Curry was told locally that the two stones had been 'used by the Danes for playing the game of *Rings*, one standing on one side and another at the opposite side and pitching the ring to each other alternately, but how the game was concluded, they do not remember'.

Pl. 24—Glencullen standing stone.

One type of monument which may date from the Iron Age is the ring-barrow. Ring-barrows occur at Ballyremon near the Great Sugar Loaf, and at Newtown Hill above Glencullen; however, neither has been excavated and their dating remains to be confirmed. They consist of a simple circular earthen mound enclosed by a ditch and an outer bank. Excavations of these monuments elsewhere in Ireland show that cremated human remains were placed near the centre of the mound, often without grave-goods or pottery.

THE ROMAN CONNECTION

Ireland was not directly affected by the Roman colonisation of neighbouring Britain. However, contacts between Roman Britain and Ireland herald the end of the prehistoric period, for the Romans were the first to make written reference to this country, though these generally fleeting remarks were not always accurate or flattering. While there is documentary evidence that the Romans considered a military expedition to Ireland, there is no conclusive evidence to indicate that they ever landed an invasion force on Irish soil. Even so, there is clear evidence for economic contacts between Ireland and Roman Britain. Indeed, any Roman sailing the Mediterranean-like shores around Dalkey, Killiney and Bray Head would immediately have been reminded of home.

In 1835, during the construction of houses at Esplanade Terrace (subsequently owned by the antiquarian Sir William Wilde) on the sea front at Bray, a cemetery was found consisting of several human skeletons in graves 'placed regularly side by side, and separated each from its neighbour by thin partitions of flag or stone'. A number of Roman coins (Hadrian, AD 117–38, and Trajan, AD 97–117) were found, lying on or beside the breast of several of the skeletons. Was this a cemetery of Roman visitors to our shores, or were these coins placed in the graves of Irish people who had made contacts with Roman Britain? Such coins had no currency value since there was no monetary system in Ireland; however, they were made of precious metals and probably also had a novelty value.

The early Middle Ages

Pl. 25—Silhouette of Kilgobban high cross.

THE DAWN OF HISTORY

By the year 400 the Roman Empire was in decline, and the Romans had lost their foothold in Britain. Despite evidence for contact with the Romans in Britain a few centuries before, it was a long time before the Irish themselves began to document the names of people and the dates of events in this country. Even then, the early history of south-east Dublin and north-east Wicklow was largely ignored by the early chroniclers—the churches are rarely mentioned, and the political leaders in secular society are even more obscure. However, occasionally we are given glimpses of life during this period, and we know that *Cualu* was an early name for the whole area of the Dublin and Wicklow mountains. There is a tradition that this area was famous for its ale, which was consumed from vessels made from the horns of a wild ox, and according to one early text 'he is not king over glorious Ireland who does not consume the ale of Cualu'. There is another tradition that the first smelting of gold in Ireland was by Tighernas and that his artificer was Uchadan of Cualu, perhaps not coincidental given the wealth of gold once available in the Wicklow Mountains.

At the dawn of history Cualu was controlled by the Dál Messin Corb, a leading tribe in Leinster; St Kevin of Glendalough, born in Kildare, was a member of this tribe. Maelodran, a legendary hero of the Dál Messin Corb, was celebrated as the slaughterer of a rival tribe, the Uí Mail, killing their warriors 'as a quern might crush corn'. Maelodran married the daughter of a rival Uí Mail king, who successfully conspired to have him killed, after which the Dál Messin Corb withdrew to the area around Arklow and the Uí Mail rose to power as kings of Leinster during the seventh century. At this time the Uí Théig became the leading tribe of north-east Wicklow and south-east Dublin. They were replaced during the eighth century by the Uí Briúin, who lent the name *Uí Briúin Cualann* to much of the territory known today as Rathdown.

Pl. 26—Sunrise and silhouette of the Great Sugar Loaf from Onagh.

OE CUALANN

In old Irish poetry this mountain was called 'the renowned, the ancient Oe Cualann'. *Cualann* was the early historic name for the territory of south-east Dublin and north-east Wicklow, while *Óe* may mean 'ear'—the pointed top of the Great Sugar Loaf may be seen to have the appearance of an animal's ear. The memory of this ancient territory may also be preserved in the name Glencullen, *Gleann Cualann*, 'the glen of Cualann'.

Pl. 27—Dalkey Island church, seen through the musket-loop of the Martello tower.

DALKEY ISLAND

From the sixth century onwards churches were founded on islands as hermitages, particularly along the western Atlantic coast of Ireland. Dalkey Island, one of the few Early Christian island churches on the east coast of Ireland, may have begun as such a hermitage during the sixth or seventh century. The church there was dedicated to St Begnet. The island is mentioned in the annals in 727, when a cow was seen with one head, three bodies, two tails and six legs, and which provided milk three times a day.

In 917 the Vikings founded a town at Dublin, and their power extended far beyond its walls. Many Viking families settled in the hinterland of Dublin, including parts of Uí Briúin Cualann. During the eleventh century their influence may have extended as far south as Delgany. During the twelfth century the Mac Torcaills were the rulers of Dublin, and members of the family had settled in parts of Glencree, Glencullen, and Tully. Sometime after 1130 the Uí Dúnchada became a powerful force in Uí Briúin Cualann, and their kings took the name MacGillaMoCholmóc. Their chief residence was at Lyons on the Dublin/Kildare border, but following the arrival of the Anglo-Normans in 1169 they took up residence in Rathdown, near Greystones.

EVIDENCE FOR THE EARLIEST CHRISTIANS

The earliest Christians arrived in Ireland nearly 400 years after the birth of Christ. In AD 431 Pope Celestine sent Palladius as the first bishop to 'the Irish believing in Christ', though the widespread conversion of the native pagan Irish has often been attributed to St Patrick, who allegedly arrived in AD 432. The conversion was probably gradual, and in the sixth century the Christian church was given new impetus when the monastic way of life became popular under the influence of many great saints, such as St Kevin, who is associated with Glendalough at the heart of the Wicklow Mountains.

Many of the churches in south-east Dublin and north-east Wicklow have early origins, though the original timber churches once forming the focus of these monasteries have long disappeared. Placenames often provide the best

Pl. 28—Incised cross at Dalkey Island.

Opposite the door of the eleventh-century church on Dalkey Island, incised on a near-vertical face of natural rock outcrop, is a ring-headed cross with slightly splayed arms, and with small bosses at the intersection of the arms. This cross may date from the eighth or ninth century.

St Corman of the Glen of the Waterfall

At the beginning of the nineteenth century there were the ruins of a church here, but today nothing remains except a boulder with four hollows (or bullauns) known as the 'Praying Stone'. This church may have been the remains of a hermitage founded by 'St Corman of the glen of the waterfall', supposedly a piper and anchorite of the eighth century. He was a friend of Maelruain (d. 792), the founder of Tallaght, who frequently sent him presents.

Pl. 29—Powerscourt Waterfall.

identification of such early churches, and preserve the names of early saints, e.g. Kilmacud (*cill McCudd*: St Macud, baptised by St Brendan in AD 547), and Taney (*teach Nathi*: St Nathi, a sixth-century bishop—the Irish word *teach*, meaning house, was commonly used to denote a church). The patron saint of Carrickbrennan (Monkstown) was St Mochonna, a sixth-century bishop of Holmpatrick, near Skerries in north County Dublin. Killcolum was the name of a church in Lackandarragh, west of Enniskerry, on the slopes of Knockree, which may have been dedicated to St Columba. Kilcrony near Bray was dedicated to St Cróne, a female saint who was allegedly related to St Columba. Killiney (*cill-inghene-Léinín*, 'the church of Léinín's daughters') was dedicated to the seven holy daughters of Léinín—Aiglend, Machain, Luiden, Druiden, Lucell, Rimtech and Brigit. Their brother, Colmán mac Léinín, was the founder of Cloyne, Co. Cork, and died in about 604. One of Léinín's daughters, Aiglend, had a son, Fintan, who may have been the St Fintan associated with the church at Clonkeen, now Kill o' the Grange. An unlocated church near

CROSS-SLABS

Pl. 30a—Cross-slab at Killegar.

Pl. 30b—Cross-slab at Whitechurch.

Pl. 31—Oldcourt cross base, east face.

Many early Irish high crosses depict events from the Scriptures, and a fine base of such a high cross from Oldcourt at Bray features several such biblical scenes. On the east face is a scene of the Last Judgement, with a winged St Michael holding weighing scales, as well as a depiction of Daniel in the Lions' Den.

A PRAYER AT DELGANY

At Delgany is the granite shaft of a ninth-century high cross. An inscription on the south face reads:

OR DO

....

OCUS

DO O

DRAN

SAIR

'A prayer for .... and for Odran the wright'

The inscription asks for a prayer for two people, but unfortunately the first name is illegible. The second person named, Odran, was a wright (*sair*)—someone who worked with wood—but he cannot be identified with certainty in the historical sources. The naming of a wood-worker on a cross may indicate that Odran's trade was specifically associated with the church, and perhaps he was a builder of wooden churches or a carver of wooden crosses.

Pl. 32—Cross shaft at Delgany.

Fig. 15—Cross-slab at Fairy Hill, Killarney, Bray.

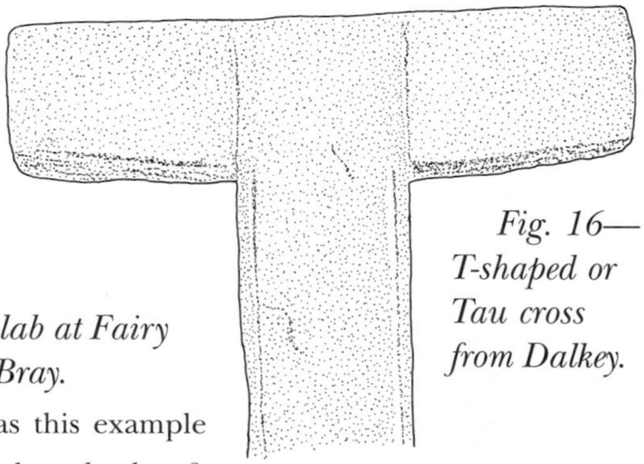

Cross-slabs, such as this example from Fairy Hill in the suburbs of Bray, were the burial memorials of early ecclesiastics. Frequently such slabs are the only visible remains of the earliest churches, and the Fairy Hill cross marks the site of a church known as Killarney, *cill escop Saran*, 'the church of Bishop Saran'.

Fig. 16—T-shaped or Tau cross from Dalkey.

Shankill was dedicated to St Comgall. There were also strong links with Wales, and the churches at Delgany, Killegar and Kilgobbin appear to have been dedicated to Welsh saints.

Many of the churches were dedicated to saints who had links with the Dál Messin Corb, a tribe powerful in Leinster until the seventh century. The church at Jamestown, originally part of Ballyogan, was dedicated to St Mochaime, a brother of St Kevin. Delgany was dedicated to St Chuaróg or Mochorog, who apparently gave the last rites to St Kevin when he died in 622. Ballyman was dedicated to St Sillán, who was an early bishop at Glendalough, and a holy well near the church was dedicated to St Kevin. St Moconnog of Kilmacanogue and St Moling (founder of Ferns), associated with a well at Kilmalin near Enniskerry, both had strong associations with Glendalough. St Berchán of the Dál Messin Corb was associated with a lost church at Shankill.

During the eighth century the Uí Briúin ruled much of south-east Dublin and north-east Wicklow. They arrived from north Kildare, bringing with them the influence of the famous monastery at Kildare founded by St Brigid around

EARLY CHRISTIAN KILLEGAR

Now in the National Museum of Ireland, this bronze-coated iron bell (20cm high) from Killegar probably dates from AD 700–900. Unfortunately the bell is quite badly corroded, and the clapper is missing. The handle is too small to fit in a person's hand, and it was probably hung on a hand-held rope.

Pl. 33—Hand-bell from Killegar (courtesy of the National Museum of Ireland ©).

AD 500. Several churches in the area have a strong association with St Brigid, including Kilbride, near Bray, and Stillorgan. The old texts tell of a visit paid to St Brigid of Kildare by eight bishops of Tully, suggesting links between the two churches. Political motives should never be underestimated within the early Irish church, which depended largely on patronage from local rulers. It appears that several Rathdown churches may have been taken over or founded by the powerful monastery of Kildare in an attempt to counteract and challenge the cult of St Kevin, which linked many of the churches with Glendalough.

Physical remains of the earliest church foundations have rarely survived. Stone churches were not constructed until the tenth and eleventh centuries, replacing their timber predecessors. Sometimes more durable stone objects survive from this period, such as cross-decorated slabs, high crosses and bullaun stones (fonts, consisting of a simple basin carved into a rough boulder), and these are frequently the only archaeological evidence illustrating the antiquity of a church.

ORGANISATION OF THE CHURCH

The organisation of the Irish church was primarily monastic. It was not until the beginning of the twelfth century that it was gradually reorganised into dioceses, and abbots were replaced by bishops. However, there is reason to believe that in south-east Dublin and north-east Wicklow these changes had taken place much earlier. For example, a holy well at Kilmalin, near Enniskerry, was dedicated to St Moling, bishop of Ferns, who died in AD 624. The old Irish name of the church at Tully was *tulach na n-Epscop*, 'the hill of the bishops'. The site of a church at Killarney, today marked by an early cross-slab, was known in Irish as *cill easpuig Sáráin*, 'the church of Bishop Saran'. On the other hand, abbots are not connected with the churches of this area, either historically or in placenames.

By the middle of the eleventh century the Viking king, Sitric Silkbeard, son of Óláf, reorganised the church in Dublin by founding a bishopric there at Christ Church, perhaps shortly after his pilgrimage to Rome in 1028. The consequences of this move must have reverberated beyond the walls of the town into the surrounding countryside. This influence is testified by the placenames of several churches, such as Balally (*baile Amhlaibh*, 'the town of Óláf'), which may have been dedicated to a Viking saint. The church at Rathmichael appears to have been dedicated to St Michael, the patron saint of seafarers. Furthermore, the fascinating range of grave-slabs known as Rathdown slabs, so called because they are only found at churches in the Barony of Rathdown, may feature abstract designs of Viking origin. Their widespread occurrence in the area highlights the role of the local Vikings in the development of the church during this period.

Pl. 34—Twelfth-century high cross at Tully.

TULLY HIGH CROSS

In a field near the church at Tully is a twelfth-century high cross depicting the bearded figure of a bishop in a full-length garment and holding a crosier. The church at Tully and the surrounding lands were granted to Christ Church in Dublin by Sitric Mac Torcaill some time before the Anglo-Norman invasion, and it is tempting to see the bishop on the high cross there as representing St Laurence O'Toole, archbishop of Dublin (1162–80), who confirmed the grant.

Pl. 35—The sun setting behind Tully high cross.

By the middle of the twelfth century the reorganisation of the Irish church into dioceses was complete, and at Tully this was celebrated on a high cross with the depiction of a bishop holding a crosier. At this time most of the local churches fell within the remit of the newly created diocese of Glendalough (which became united to that of Dublin in 1214). Stillorgan can be translated as *teach Lorcán*, the 'house (church) of Laurence', and may refer to St Laurence O'Toole, bishop of Glendalough from 1153 to 1162, when he became archbishop of Dublin until his death in Normandy in November 1180.

GRAVE-SLABS

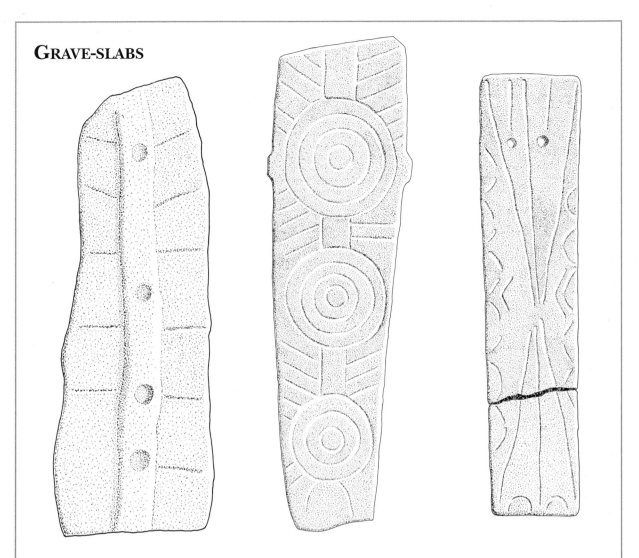

Fig. 17—Rathdown slabs from Rathmichael, Rathfarnham and Tully (after Breen 1981 and Ó hÉailidhe 1957).

Rathdown slabs feature a distinctive type of decoration not found elsewhere in Christian Ireland. They are found at the church sites throughout this area, for example at Ballyman, Dalkey, Kilgobbin, Killegar, Kiltiernan, Rathfarnham, Rathmichael, Tully and Whitechurch. No two slabs are the same, but there is generally a repetition of motifs. The most common decorations include a herringbone design and cupmarks, often enclosed by concentric circles, and are based on local Viking art styles. Frequently the decoration on these slabs does not fit readily within the traditional range of Christian symbols, but the meaning of any special symbolism has been lost over time. When a cross does feature on these slabs it generally takes the form of a saltire cross, such as that found on the slab from Rathfarnham, which is so elongated that it is no longer recognisable as a cross.

THE EARLIEST STONE CHURCHES

The earliest churches were probably made of timber and, as might be expected, have not survived. However, their memory is preserved by placenames such as *Dair Teach,* 'oak house or oratory', the name of a church mentioned in the old texts as near Bray. The original name of Whitechurch was *cill Fhuinseann,* which may refer to an early church there of ash wood.

Many ancient stone churches are scattered throughout south-east Dublin and north-east Wicklow. These replaced the earlier timber oratories and the earliest can be dated to around the eleventh century. They were rectangular buildings with a flat lintelled door at the west end and a small window at the east end, lighting the altar. Often they feature antae, whereby the long walls

Pls 36–7—Dalkey Island church (top), and doorway of Killiney church (bottom).

EARLY CHURCH ARCHITECTURE

The church on Dalkey Island, dedicated to St Begnet and featuring antae and a flat-lintelled west doorway, represents a classic example of eleventh-century Irish church architecture. The bellcote on the west gable is a late medieval addition.

The western doorway of the church at Killiney is typical of the earliest stone churches in Ireland, constructed with inclining jambs and a large, flat slab forming a lintel. The soffit of the lintel features a carving of a Greek cross.

THE HIGH CROSS

High crosses, such as those found at Tully, were frequently commissioned by an abbot or a local ruler. They were placed around the church, symbolising and celebrating the sanctity of the monastery. Overlooking the lane to the church at Tully is a ringed high cross, possibly dating from the early tenth century. The top is in the shape of a gable roof with finials and shingles. In *Grose's Antiquities of Ireland* (1796) Edward Ledwich wrote: 'One cross mounted on a pedastal has four perforations in its hands, through which child-bed linen was drawn to secure easy delivery, and health to the infant. These holes were also used in matrimonial contracts among the Northerns settled here; the parties joining hands through them, and no engagement was thought more solemn or binding.'

extend beyond the gable walls, carrying the roof beyond the gable ends of the building. The capstone of a tenth-century high cross at Tully depicts the high-pitched slated roof with finials of such early buildings. Early stone churches survive at Dalkey Island, Kilcrony and Kill o' the Grange, but the many alterations made by subsequent generations often makes it difficult to identify the earliest structural remains. It was not until the twelfth century that the earliest stone arches were used in Irish churches, particularly to construct graceful rounded arches, such as the tiny example at Killiney, separating the nave from the small chancel. These arches were mimicked by the lintels of windows, which were rounded in shape, sometimes carved from a single piece of stone.

Some early Irish monastic sites had majestic belfries known as round towers,

Pl. 38—High cross at Tully.

ROMANESQUE ARCHITECTURE

The twelfth century brought a reorganisation of the church and with this came a new type of architecture, known as Romanesque. In its simplest form Romanesque architecture favoured the use of round arches, often mimicked by round-headed

windows, as at Tully. The round chancel arch at Tully was used to separate the earlier church from the newly constructed eastward extension, which served as a chancel, while the earlier building became the nave.

Pls 39–40—Chancel arch at Tully (top). Round-headed windows at Tully (bottom).

which were the tallest buildings of their day, equivalent to modern sky-scrapers. They symbolised a reaching up to heaven, and would have impressed upon local communities the power of the church. The use of mortar and their basic circular tapering form meant that these towers were exceptionally well designed, as testified by the many that are still standing 900 years later. We will never know how tall the round tower at Rathmichael once stood; like many others around the country, it may have been severely damaged by storm or lightning.

The early churches were often enclosed by circular stone and earthen ramparts, which defined the consecrated ground around the central oratory. These have rarely survived the passage of time, though the original

Pl. 41—Church at Kiltiernan.

RATHDOWN MASON?

The Fassaroe cross lends its name to a small series of distinctive granite crosses which were probably all the work of the same stonemason, who worked at several churches in Rathdown around the middle of the twelfth century. Four others are known—at Blackrock, Killegar, Rathmichael and Shankill—and they have been compared with crosses from Cornwall in south-west England. These are generally quite short granite crosses, with the exception of the tall cross at Fassaroe. The cross heads are mostly wheel-shaped, featuring a simple though distinctive type of Crucifixion scene in false relief.

Pl. 42—Fassaroe cross.

BOUNDARY MARKER

The Fassaroe-type cross beside an old lane in Rathmichael may mark a route or a boundary between the churches at Kiltuck and Rathmichael. The granite cross, set in an uncarved boulder base, is unusual in that there is a Crucifixion scene on both faces, depicted here in high relief. Otherwise the Rathmichael cross has a typical wheel-shaped head with short projecting arms, which also feature on the cross at Shankill (originally from Kiltuck).

Pl. 43—The Rathmichael cross.

Pl. 44—Carved head on cross from Kiltuck.

ecclesiastical enclosure can still be seen at Rathmichael. Today, the peaceful ruins of these early churches disguise what were originally busy centres of learning, crafts, industry and trade.

DEFENDED SETTLEMENTS

During this period many Irish farmers felt it necessary to defend their farmsteads within ringforts. Ringforts consist of a circular area enclosed by a large earthen bank, with a deep outer ditch to provide the material for the bank and to create an obstacle for attackers. An example of a ringfort can be found at Annacrivey, between Enniskerry and Glencree. It consists of a roughly circular area, 21m across, enclosed by an earth and stone bank 2–5m wide and in places over 1m high. There are traces of an outer ditch and the entrance was at the north. In some areas the builders opted for stone forts, known as cashels,

Fig. 18— Reconstruction of a ringfort (oil painting by Catherine Geraghty, 1997).

RINGFORTS

Ringforts were the partially defended farmsteads of wealthy farmers, built between 600 and 900. Within the ringfort or cashel the farmer built his timber house, typically round in plan. Some of the smaller farm animals may have been kept within the enclosure, and several excavated examples elsewhere in the country have shown that metal-working, glass-working and other craft industries, such as textile manufacture, took place within ringforts.

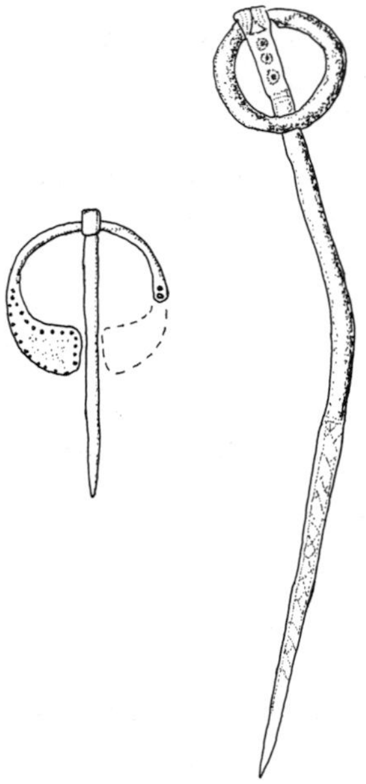

Fig. 19—Brooch and ring-pin from Dalkey Island (after Liversage 1968).

PERSONAL ADORNMENT

Among the objects recovered during the excavations of the promontory fort on Dalkey Island were this brooch and ring-pin, both dating from the seventh or eighth century. The brooch consists of a flattened tinned or silvered penannular ring (3.5cm in diameter) with expanded terminals at each end, but one of the terminals is missing. The surviving terminal is bordered by a row of small punch-marks on the front face. The bronze ring-pin is 14.7cm long, and the shaft is flattened and decorated with a mixture of a lightly incised step pattern and hatching. The pin head is decorated with a dot-in-circle motif.

such as at Ballybrew, overlooking the Glencullen River valley. This consists of a collapsed drystone wall averaging 2m in width and enclosing an oval area measuring 35m east–west by 29m north–south. Almost at the very centre and summit of the prehistoric hillfort at Rathmichael are the collapsed remains of another cashel, probably built long after the hillfort had fallen out of use.

That Rathdown must have been a densely populated area is indicated by the number of church sites. It is surprising, therefore, that there is not greater evidence for secular settlement in the form of ringforts. Perhaps there was no need for such a large number of defended settlements as in other areas of the country, for Rathdown was out of reach of the constant attention of both the kings of Meath to the north of the Viking town of Dublin and the kings of Leinster to the west of the Wicklow Mountains. Alternatively, the scarcity of ringforts may be explained by other factors; Scott, writing in 1913, claimed that 'You can count no less than ten raths on Killegar townland, though I may tell you that some of them are easier to recognise on the map than on the ground. Partly through the action of natural forces, but much more as a result of agricultural operations, the old raths are slowly but surely disappearing.' The local superstition that explained ringforts as the abodes of the fairies did not preserve these sites as elsewhere in Ireland. Many ringforts in the Rathdown area have probably been removed from the landscape since the twelfth century, when the arrival of the Anglo-Normans with their new techniques of warfare rendered the ringfort obsolete.

Another form of defended settlement site constructed at this time was the promontory fort on Dalkey Island. This consisted of a steep-sided ditch over 2m deep and 5m wide, the material from which was used to construct an equally substantial bank, cutting off and defending the northern tip of the island. The bank sealed a type of pottery known as E-ware (which probably contained imported wine from Britain or France), indicating that the fortification was built shortly after the seventh–eighth century. The excavation recovered a wealth of other finds, including several ring-pins, a brooch and a fragment of an early glass vessel. The dimensions suggest that this earthwork was intended to be a defensive structure, but the evidence for the accumulation of rubbish in the ditch, which served to make it less effective, suggests that the threats which provided the incentive to construct the fortification had subsided.

VIKINGS

The Vikings are traditionally seen as raiders and plunderers of Irish churches, and there is a tradition that the rich shrine which contained the relics of St Mochonna, associated with a church at Carrickbrennan (Monkstown), was among the first treasures to be taken away during the Viking raid at Holmpatrick, near Skerries, at the end of the eighth century. In 939 Coibhdeanach, abbot of Cill-achaidh (Killeigh, Co. Offaly), drowned at Dalkey while fleeing from the 'foreigners'. It has been suggested that the promontory fort on Dalkey Island was used by the Vikings as a detention camp for slaves, and Abbot Coibhdeanach may have been fleeing from rather than to the island. For many years the Vikings were seen as destructive elements in Irish society. Certainly the antiquarians of the last century did not speak favourably of them, and Wakeman blamed them for the damage to the crosses from Kill o' the Grange. However, we should not blame all atrocities on the Vikings, and we should never underestimate their influence and accomplishments in Ireland.

The Vikings, or Ostmen as they called themselves, were quick to see the economic potential of settling in Ireland, where there were no towns or ports. They were the first to establish urban centres in Ireland, which were to become (and continue to be) important centres of trade and industry. The Vikings acted as middlemen between the native royal families of the Irish midlands and the commercial markets of Britain and mainland Europe. The most important of these towns in the east of Ireland was Dublin, founded in 917. Archaeological excavations in the city centre have yielded tremendous evidence for the development and wealth of this town. Therefore it can only be expected that the development of Viking Dublin as a town and international port must have had far-reaching implications for its hinterland, known as *Dyflinarskiri*, which extended as far south as Delgany and Greystones. Many Ostmen settled in this

RATHDOWN SLABS

Pl. 45—Rathdown slab at Killegar.

The unusual, almost pagan, decoration of Rathdown slabs, such as these examples from Killegar and Whitechurch, led early antiquarians to argue that they must be pre-Christian. However, today they are generally regarded as having been influenced by Viking art styles and as representing the burials of local Viking Christians. Ragnvald, son of Óláf Cuarán, king of Dublin died in the Battle of Tara in

Pl. 46—Rathdown slab at Whitechurch.

980, and in that year Óláf abdicated in order to join the monastery at Iona, off the coast of Scotland. Clearly the Vikings of Dublin had converted to Christianity by this time. The widespread occurrence of Rathdown slabs at so many churches throughout south-east Dublin and neighbouring parts of County Wicklow illustrates the extent of Viking settlement in this area and their influence on local churches.

Fig. 20—Coin of Eadgar from Dalkey.

COIN HOARD

In 1838 a hoard of over 70 Anglo-Saxon coins was found during the construction of the Concert Hall of the Queen's Royal Hotel at Dalkey. Many of the coins feature Eadgar, an Anglo-Saxon king who ruled from 959 to 975. The coins probably reached Ireland as a result of trade between Dublin and Chester. Michael Dolley put forward the fascinating suggestion that the hoard may have been left unrecovered by an Ostman killed at the Battle of Tara, fought between the Dublin Ostmen and the Irish under Máel Sechnaill in 980.

area, and by 980 many had converted to Christianity. Those living in Dublin town needed food and raw materials, such as timber, for their thriving industries. This brought much wealth to the hinterland south of Dublin port, and encouraged the growth of many pre-existing church foundations and the construction of several new churches throughout the area. In this way the Vikings, who had originally brought so much destruction to churches, now brought tremendous wealth.

For the most part, Viking settlement in north-east Wicklow and south-east Dublin thrived because it was sheltered by the Wicklow Mountains from attacks by the powerful Kildare tribes to the west, and the town of Dublin provided a barrier of a different sort to the powerful tribes of Meath to the north. However, the relationship between the Dublin Vikings and the native Irish rulers of Meath and Leinster was not always amicable. In 942 the Irish tribes of Leinster attacked and burned Dublin, and a number of the inhabitants escaped the carnage by fleeing in their ships to Dalkey Island. Sitric Silkbeard, son of Óláf, king of Dublin, was defeated at Delgany by Owgaire, king of Leinster, in 1021. This battle was accompanied by a slaughter of the 'foreigners' in Rathdown. Perhaps a silver finger-ring from Killincarrig near Delgany was lost at this battle. Along the band of this ring are traces of a runic inscription, and the plate is decorated with silver filigree.

However, the lasting impression the Vikings have left on many of the placenames of Rathdown suggests that the Scandinavians became well integrated within the local community, and played an active role in shaping the future of that society. The church of Stagonil (near Powerscourt) may incorporate the Norse woman's name Gunnhildr, and Ballaly incorporates the name *Amhlaibh*, Irish for the Viking name Óláf. Other placenames include Windgates and nearby Coolagad, which preserve the Norse word for street, *gata*. The Irish word for island, *inis*, was replaced by the Norse word *eye*, changing *Deilginis* into *Dalkeye*. Curtlestown near Glencree preserves the name Mac Torcaill, associated with some of the twelfth-century rulers of Viking Dublin. A now-obsolete placename for part of Bellevue Demesne near Delgany, Ballygunner, preserves the Norse name Gunnarr. The church at Rathmichael appears to represent a dedication to St Michael, who was the patron saint of seafarers among the Ostmen. MacDoyle of Rathmichael was an Ostman mentioned in connection with the records of the archbishop's court at Shankill at the beginning of the thirteenth century. This clearly indicates that the Norse of Dublin had settled outside the city, as rural farmers. Doyle, a common local family name, is an Anglicisation of the Irish *dubh gall*, which translates as 'dark foreigner', a name given to the Scandinavian inhabitants of the area. By the end of the twelfth century the Vikings became overshadowed by the arrival of a new political and social force in Ireland, the Anglo-Normans.

The later Middle Ages

A FORGOTTEN GHOST

Puck's Castle at Rathmichael broods rather menacingly over the landscape, so the interpretation that the puck referred to is a *puca* that once haunted the residence is easy to believe. The castle is in fact an unfortified house of late sixteenth-century date.

Pl. 47—Puck's Castle.

THE NORMAN CONQUEST

By the middle of the twelfth century Ireland's ports, in particular Dublin and Waterford, had established significant trade and political links with England, and also with mainland Europe. Ultimately these new links led to the arrival of the Anglo-Normans in 1169, initially at the invitation of the dethroned Leinster king Diarmait MacMurrough. At this time (and for nearly a century before) the ruling clans of Rathdown were the MacGillaMoCholmóc family in north-east Wicklow and the Mac Torcaill family in south-east Dublin. With the arrival of

Strongbow in August 1170 the Norman interest in Ireland became transformed into an official conquest. The Mac Torcaills, who owned much of south-east Dublin, were also the rulers of Dublin itself when the Normans attacked the town, and contemporary Norman commentators referred to their leader, Askluluv Mac Torcaill, as a traitor and deceiver.

In September 1170 Raymond le Gros and Miles de Cogan led the attack on Dublin. Domnall MacGillaMoCholmóc remained neutral during the battle, perhaps out of loyalty to his overlord, Diarmait MacMurrough (though in 1141 Diarmait had blinded one of his relatives, Muircertach MacGillaMoCholmóc), and there can be no doubt that he had little sympathy for the Viking rulers of Dublin. Contemporary accounts suggest that Domnall made an agreement with Miles de Cogan and lay in wait with his followers, slaughtering those Ostmen who fled from the victorious Normans. Others fled by sea to the Isle of Man. Shortly afterwards the Ostmen returned and laid siege to the Normans in Dublin. However, they were taken by surprise by Richard de Cogan, brother of Miles, and in the battle Walter de Ridelesford killed one of their leaders, John the Wode ('the impetuous').

In 1171 Rory O'Conor, high king of Ireland, camped at Castleknock and laid siege to the Normans in Dublin. He was helped by Murchad MacMurrough, who, unlike his recently deceased brother Diarmait, had little sympathy for the Normans and who set up camp at Dalkey. It appears that Domnall MacGillaMoCholmóc switched his loyalty to his Irish comrades and joined the siege of Dublin. However, the siege failed, and Strongbow's possessions became secure.

REDISTRIBUTION OF LANDS

Shortly afterwards King Henry II arrived in Ireland (1171), worried about Strongbow's speedy ascent to power. The king granted the kingdom of Leinster to Richard the Earl (Strongbow), reserving Dublin for himself. One of those who received an extensive grant from Strongbow in 1173 as a knight's fee for his part in the Conquest was a Yorkshire man, Walter de Ridelesford, a councillor of Strongbow and known to his peers as a brave and noble warrior. Among his grants were lands in Kildare, much of the territory formerly known as Uí Briúin Cualann, including Bray, and the manor of Thorncastle, now Booterstown. He was a man with important friends, and his wife, Amabilia, was a sister of Myler FitzHenry (justiciar of Ireland from 1199 to 1208), whose father was the illegitimate son of Henry I. After his death in about 1200, Walter's daughter Basilia married Richard de Cogan; Cookstown, near Enniskerry, was formerly known as Balicogan, having been granted by Walter de Ridelesford II to de Cogan on his marriage to Basilia.

However, when Sir Walter de Ridelesford I wished to have his lands confirmed by Henry II, there appeared to be some confusion as to exactly what

Fig. 21—Bronze spearhead and brooch.

CASTLE ARTEFACTS

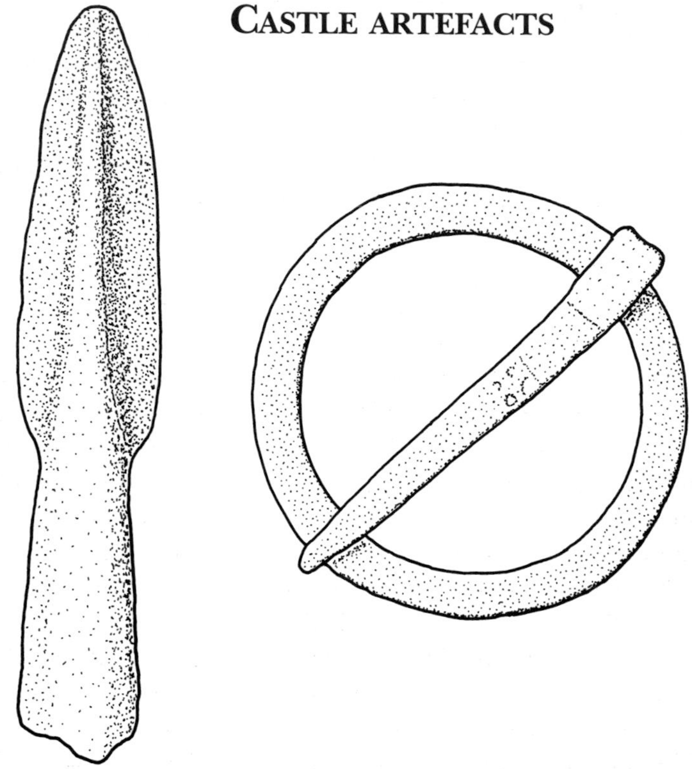

A bronze spearhead and brooch found at the site of the MacGillaMoCholmóc castle at Rathdown near Greystones.

he had originally been granted by Strongbow. There are suggestions of crooked dealing on the part of the king, who took back many of the lands originally granted to Walter I and kept for himself those lands near Dublin. Among these were Powerscourt, Ballycorus and Kiltiernan, which became part of the royal demesne of Obrun, and the manor of Thorncastle, now Booterstown. De Ridelesford's son, Walter II, became his heir around 1200. One of Walter II's daughters, Emeline, married Hugh de Lacy II, earl of Ulster, and later married Stephen de Longespée, justiciar of Ireland, whose father, William Longespée, was an illegitimate son of Henry II. When Walter II applied to Henry II to confirm the lands which he had inherited from his father, the king replied by reclaiming further lands from de Ridelesford.

The royal demesne of Obrun included parts of Ballycorus, Kiltiernan, Powerscourt and Corke, near Bray. In 1222 Geoffrey de Tureville, then archdeacon of Dublin and chancellor of Ireland, leased the manor from the king. The king also established a royal forest in the Wicklow Mountains at Glencree, which may have included Knockree (King's Hill). Perhaps there was already a forest here, established by the Vikings to provide wood for their industry and port at Dublin. In 1244 a royal order was issued to the justiciar of Chester to use Dalkey as a harbour in order to send 60 does and 20 bucks to stock the royal forest at Glencree. In 1290 timber works were established by Queen Eleanor at Glencree, and shortly afterwards John de Wallope used timber from the forest to built a house at Ballycorus. A second royal forest, called Garfloun, was located in the Obrun demesne, somewhere between Powerscourt and Kilmacanogue, perhaps in Charleville Demesne, the old name of which was *coill mhór*, 'the great wood'. In 1237 Garfloun was leased from the king by Geoffrey de Tureville, archbishop of Dublin.

Unusually for a Gaelic lord, Domnall MacGillaMoCholmóc remained an important landowner, largely because of his marriage to Dervorgilla, the daughter of Diarmait MacMurrough, which made him Strongbow's brother-in-law. Despite having joined the Irish siege against the Normans at Dublin in 1171, Domnall submitted to Henry II on his arrival in Ireland. He was allowed to retain the lands at Rathdown, near Greystones, where he had his principal residence. Kilruddery also remained in his possession; his son, Diarmait, granted land in Kilruddery to Richard de Felda in return for a pair of gilt spurs to be presented to him and his heirs each year at Michaelmas. The name Giltspur is still used for the area between the foot of the Little Sugar Loaf and Kilruddery House. In 1207 Diarmait's own fee for holding the entire land grant from King John was the service of one knight. In 1227 his son, John Fitzdermot (Domnall MacGillaMoCholmóc's grandson), was summoned to serve as a knight in King Henry III's army. He married Claricia, daughter of Gilbert FitzGriffin, who was a nephew of that Raymond le Gros who had led the Norman attack on Dublin. In this way the family became part of the Anglo-Norman establishment. In 1278 John's grandson, Ralph, was paid the sum of £4. 9s. 8d. by the Dublin exchequer for expenses incurred in guarding the borders of the 'vales of Dublin' against the Irish clans. At the beginning of the fourteenth century the MacGillaMoCholmócs, or FitzDermots as they had come to be known, relinquished their lordship; however, up to the fifteenth century a Dublin street and gate were named after the family.

THE CHURCH

The greatest landowner within the new regime was the archbishop of Dublin, who retained those lands owned since before the Invasion, including Dalkey, Rathmichael and Shankill, as well as Stagonil (part of Powerscourt) and nearby Kilmalin. Christ Church, then the Priory of the Holy Trinity, established a manor at Clonkeen (Kill o' the Grange), lands which it already held before the Invasion. The Priory also held lands at Killiney, Loughlinstown and

KILL O' THE GRANGE

The Priory of the Holy Trinity established a manor at Kill o' the Grange, then called Clonkeen. Owing to an increase in population after the Norman Conquest it was necessary to enlarge existing church buildings in order to meet the demands of a larger congregation. At the beginning of the thirteenth century the church at Kill o' the Grange was enlarged by the insertion of an arch into the east gable of the eleventh-century church and the addition of a chancel onto the east end. A bellcote was also added to the west gable of the older building, which became the nave of the new church. Today the older church has outlived its thirteenth-century extension which, except for the east gable, has collapsed.

Pl. 48—The church at Kill o' the Grange.

Shanganagh. The Cistercian monks of St Mary's Abbey at Dublin established a grange at Carrickbrennan (Monkstown), which had also been held by the Abbey since before the Invasion.

The Dublin monastic orders also received land grants from the new landowners: for example, opposite the castle in Bray, Walter de Ridelesford II granted the Abbey of St Thomas and St Mary's Abbey separate plots on the river from which to ship commodities, in particular timber, to their monasteries in Dublin. The grange of Clonkeen (Kill o' the Grange) also held land and a mill beside the river at Bray. Whitechurch and Harold's Grange were granted by David de St Michael and Milo de Stanton to St Mary's. Lands in Glencullen were granted to St Mary's *c.* 1213 by Richard de Cogan, who also donated lands at Ballybrew to St Thomas's Abbey. About this time Richard de Felda granted

Pl. 49—Church at Newcourt, Bray Head.

THE LITTLE FORT OF THE BELL

On the slopes of Bray Head, with a commanding view northwards across the bay towards Killiney headland and Dalkey Island, are the ruins of an early thirteenth-century church known by the curious name of *Rathín a chluig*, the 'little fort of the bell'. The Archbolds granted the church to the Friary of Augustinian Hermits.

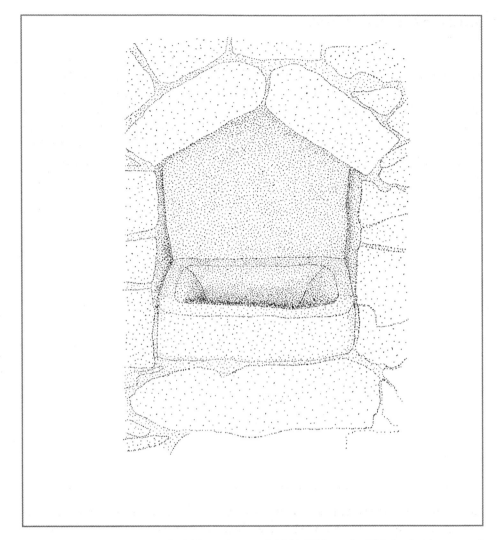

Fig. 22—Holy water stoup at Dalkey.

Kilruddery to St Thomas's Abbey. Around 1200 Walter de Ridelesford granted several of the Bray churches, as well as Kilmacud, to the Priory of Graney, in Kildare. Lands in Rathmichael and Old Connaught, including the church at Ballyman, were granted by William Lisbon to the Knights Templar. The Priory of All Hallows received lands called 'Balyofyn' adjoining Kilgobbin and Ballyogan from Claricia, wife of John FitzDermot, *c.* 1235, and around this time the nuns of Lismullen, Co. Meath, were granted lands at Cornelscourt and Cabinteely. The Leper Hospital of St Stephen in Dublin was granted lands called 'Balygyregan' by Geoffrey Tyrel and his wife Sara. The lands subsequently became known as Leperstown, though there is no evidence to show that the hospital ever had an auxiliary home for lepers here.

ANGLO-NORMAN SOCIETY

The Anglo-Normans were responsible for bringing about a complete reorganisation of Irish society. They built large and imposing stone castles to consolidate their grants, and established manors and boroughs with their own markets and currency, as well as founding several new parish churches. Castles were the strength behind the Anglo-Norman conquest, and soon became the centres of Anglo-Norman rule. Some of the earliest castles were of timber, though today only the earthworks of these survive. The more important castles, and those which were properly funded, were of stone, such as Dundrum.

Pl. 50—Silver penny of Edward II (1307–27) from Templecarrig Lower, near Greystones.

Generally the earliest castles consisted of a keep or donjon which was the main residence of the lord. Around this keep was a courtyard or bailey, enclosed by a bawn wall, within which the garrison of soldiers could be housed. Some castles have just faded out of existence, being replaced by later fortified buildings, such as at Shankill. Several castles were built at towns, for example Bray (built sometime before 1225), whereas others, such as Rathdown Upper near Greystones, had a rural setting. However, even these rural castles were not altogether isolated. Nothing remains today of the cabins, outhouses and industrial buildings, such as mills, that would have formed a village nearby.

The Anglo-Normans established a highly organised system of agriculture, based on both pasture and cultivation. In 1330 wheat, barley, oats, beans and peas were harvested at Kill o' the Grange. The grange relied heavily on hired labour, and up to 34 reapers were employed during the harvest season at 1d. a day. Several new towns were established at this time, including Bray, which became a borough in 1213. Walter de Ridelesford II was granted a licence by King John for a market every Thursday at Bray, and its citizens were permitted

DUNDRUM CASTLE

The present castle at Dundrum, built by Richard Fitzwilliam around 1590, replaces an earlier castle, possibly built around the turn of the thirteenth century by the Norman knight John de Clahull, marshal of the lordship of Leinster. Recent excavations by Elizabeth O'Brien revealed evidence for the earlier castle and an elaborate gatehouse served by a drawbridge which spanned a deep moat. The later castle continued to be inhabited throughout the early eighteenth century, and this drawing, published in *The Literary and Masonic Magazine*, shows the building still roofed in 1802.

Fig. 23—Dundrum Castle in 1802, from a plate in The Literary and Masonic Magazine.

to catch hares and foxes in the king's forest. A mill once stood below the castle, beside the River Dargle, and in 1284 is mentioned in connection with a 'Robert the Baker'. Apparently there was also a fishing community in Bray, and on one occasion a fine was imposed on the inhabitants of the town because a shipwreck was concealed and the victims of the wreck buried without an inquest. Obviously the fishermen had hoped to keep the valuable wreckage for themselves.

The original settlement known as Shankill was located about 2km to the west of today's village. A fifteenth-century tower-house marks the site of a castle built by the archbishop of Dublin, Henry de Loundres (of London), sometime after 1216. The manor, probably founded at this time, began as a settlement of considerable importance, and served as one of the archbishop's principal residences in south Dublin. Furthermore, the archbishop's seneschal occasionally held court here. The archbishop was particularly interested in the value of local timber supplies, and in 1229 permission was given to clear woodland on the manor. Shortly afterwards two carpenters were killed by a fall of timber at Shankill. The town was enclosed by a wall, and access was by a great straight road which led to a gate. Around 1260 an Englishman was brought to trial for murdering the miller, an Irishman, at the gate of the town. During the 1270s Shankill was a productive manor, but only twenty years later it was in decline. There is now no trace of the original castle or the adjacent village and watermill.

THE GAELIC REVIVAL

A basic weakness of the Conquest was that there had been no concept of a frontier, or at the very least a border, with the native Irish, making it very difficult to prevent or defend against Gaelic attack on the Anglo-Norman lands. Another problem was that the new Norman landlords were often absentees and many of the native Irish had remained working the lands which they had previously owned. It was easy for the Irish tenants to revolt against their new landlords, who in their absence could not enforce the rule of law. Gradually the situation got out of control, and the Norman estates, including those owned by the archbishop and the various monasteries, were losing profits.

Matters came to a head during the Bruce invasion of Ireland in 1316, and the native Irish were quick to take advantage of the new instability of Norman rule. This heralded the Gaelic Revival, and the Wicklow Mountains, known as a 'land of war', became the home of Gaelic resurgence under the O'Toole and O'Byrne families, who for the next 300 years terrorised the countryside almost up to the gates of Dublin. Even the archbishop's manor at Shankill, which was relatively close to the centre of Anglo-Norman control at Dublin, would appear to have been deserted by 1326, when it was described thus: 'There are no buildings at Senekyll; once there were but they are now burned and thrown down by Irish felons'. Furthermore, 'Certain burgagers at Senekille, holding 17 burgages, used to pay 17s. 1¼d., now nothing because the burgagers have fled from that country on account of the Irish'.

Many of the Norman landlords could no longer afford to run their estates, and those owned by the archbishop and the monasteries were leased out to retainers on condition that they defend them from the Irish. Elsewhere the king was forced to take possession of lands and post garrisons of soldiers there to defend them. Among these were Bray and Powerscourt, which had suffered greatly at the hands of the O'Tooles and O'Byrnes. Landowners closer to Dublin often had to provide military service to the government, and in 1349 the grange at Clonkeen (Kill o' the Grange) provided two mailed horsemen and six hobelars (light cavalry) for the garrison at Bray. Such cavalry were valuable, since a problem at that time was a lack of horses with which to chase

SHANKILL CASTLE

Marking the site of the archbishop's manor is a tower-house, probably constructed during the first half of the fifteenth century, perhaps by the Barnewalls, who took over the estate from the Lawless family. The tower was refurbished in the sixteenth century, and continued to be inhabited until the middle of the eighteenth. At the end of the eighteenth century a new, more comfortable house was built adjacent to the tower.

Fig. 24—Water-colour of Shankill Castle by James Saunders, 1797 (courtesy of Andrew Bonar Law).

the Irish back into the mountains. In 1355 an unsuccessful garrison at Bray had to be replaced by chosen mounted men-at-arms, twenty light horsemen and forty archers, under the command of Sir John de Bermingham. At this time the castle at Powerscourt was in ruins and its lands, dangerously close to the colony, came under the control of the O'Tooles. However, on 11 July 1402 the citizens of Dublin, headed by John Drake (lord mayor of Dublin), successfully repulsed an attack by a force led by Donnacha O'Byrne at Ravenswell in Bray, allegedly slaying 493 of the enemy. It seems that O'Byrne had hired a band of mercenaries from Ikerrin (Tipperary) for the purpose of settling in this area and extending his land into Delgany and Bray. In 1428 the viceroy mustered a force of Dublin men at Bray and led an expedition against the O'Byrnes, equipped with axes, sickles and shovels. Despite these successes, the Irish of the mountains continued to launch regular attacks on the colony, and in 1440 the O'Byrnes plundered and burned the goods of the farmers at Kilgobbin.

KINDLESTOWN

Pl. 51—Kindlestown Castle.

At Kindlestown are the ruins of a hall-house castle which takes its name from Albert de Kenley, sheriff of Kildare, who reputedly built it in 1301.

Fig. 25—Sixteenth-century finger-ring from Kindlestown (courtesy of the National Museum of Ireland ©).

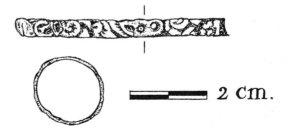

2 cm.

THE PALE

With the Gaelic Revival there came a realisation among the Norman colonists that there was a frontier. This became known as the Pale, and basically defined the hinterland around the centre of Anglo-Norman rule at Dublin. During the fifteenth century the 'Subsidised Castles Act' provided grants of £10 to encourage the construction of castles to defend the Pale and its hinterland, which became a buffer zone known as 'the march'. In Rathdown many of the upstanding castles, known more specifically as tower-houses, date from this period.

Pl. 52—Kilgobbin Castle.

Tower-houses were often built to a standard plan: rectangular, three storeys

TOWER-HOUSES

Kilgobbin Castle, probably constructed by a member of the Walsh family, is a classic example of a fifteenth-century fortified residence called a tower-house. Many tower-houses were funded by the 'Subsidised Castles Act', which provided a grant of £10 for construction costs. In 1780 Austin Cooper was able to climb the stairs up to the battlements that surrounded the roof. At the south-east corner he described a room in one of the turrets with a 'little Closet with a Nich in it from which there is a hole down to the Ground. I imagine it to have been a Necessary [toilet]'. Today the north and east walls of Kilgobbin Castle have largely collapsed, and a report in the *Dublin Penny Journal* in 1834 suggests that the walls were undermined by people who misguidedly sought the treasure of the mythical ancient Irish builder, the Goban Saor.

WINDOWS

Castle windows were small in order to retain heat and keep out the damp; even so, they were dark and cold places in which to live. Some tower-houses feature specially carved windows known as ogee-headed windows, such as can be seen on the gatehouse at Monkstown overlooking the courtyard of the castle.

Pl. 53—Window at Monkstown.

high with a stone vault over the ground floor, and topped with a steeply pitched slate or thatch roof. The roof was protected by a battlemented parapet, sometimes featuring a machicolation, which projects from or overhangs the parapet directly above the doorway so that objects could safely be dropped on assailants. Features typically found on tower-houses in the greater Dublin area are projecting turrets or towers containing a stone spiral stair, and garderobes (the medieval toilet).

The Pale was also strengthened in another way. In 1494 an act of parliament required landowners to construct a line of defences along the borders of the Pale, though there is reason to believe that not all landowners fulfilled this obligation. The best-preserved stretch is at Ballyogan, where it survives for 500m and consists of a flat-topped earthen bank (2–3m wide at the top) presently standing to 2.5m above the bottoms of the wide ditches that flank either side. The earthwork formed a defensive line between the castles at

ETERNAL VIGILANCE

Gazing in the direction of Dalkey village, this carved stone head on Bullock Castle would have kept a watchful and protective eye on those travelling to and from Dublin, and observed arrivals and departures at the nearby port.

Pl. 54—Carved head at Bullock Castle.

Kilgobbin and Carrickmines, both owned at the time by members of the Walsh family. The castle at Carrickmines was almost totally destroyed in 1641, but in the fifteenth century it was a strong castle defended by a bawn. Nearby was a hamlet called Ballinrow and a watermill. Another portion of the Pale ditch survives in Balally, which had been granted to William Walsh in 1407 on condition that he build a castle there.

The borderland area outside the Pale was known as the Marches, and during the fourteenth century these lands were occupied by the Lawless family (Shankill, Shanganagh), the Archbolds (the lands from Bray to Delgany, and Lehaunstown) and the Harolds (Rathfarnham, Whitechurch, Kilmashogue and

Kilgobbin). They were granted these lands by the king and the archbishop on the condition that they took up residence there and defended them from the Irish. Thus the king attempted to overcome the problems caused by absenteeism during the thirteenth century. The Archbolds and Harolds continued to occupy this land throughout the fifteenth and sixteenth centuries, by which time the Walsh family controlled much of the March, e.g. Ballyman, Killincarrig, Oldcourt, Corke (near Bray) and Shanganagh, as well as lands on the border of the Pale, such as Carrickmines, Kilgobbin, Balally, and even within the Pale, at Dalkey.

These families, previously owing allegiance to the Crown, gradually became less loyal. In 1462 three members of the Harold family imprisoned the archbishop of Dublin, and in the following year they attacked Dundrum Castle, killing eight of the king's lieges, driving off 600 cows, 40 plough horses and 100 sheep. In 1556 the Archbolds were suspected of collusion in the murder of Peter Talbot, owner of Fassaroe Castle. Ten years later the Archbolds were engaging in open warfare against the government forces when they attacked the garrison at Bullock. In 1566 William McShane Walsh of Corke was arrested at Old Connaught. He was alleged to have robbed a widow, Gormla O'Clondowil, in Glencullen of a brass pan, two gallons of butter, three sheep, a night-gown, two women's gowns and a cloak. While in the custody of the sub-sheriff of Dublin, William Walsh was rescued near Shanganagh by his friends, John Walsh of Shanganagh, James Goodman of Loughlinstown and Edmund Walsh of Corke. Later Walsh and his accomplices received a pardon, as a gesture of appeasement, for the administration had enough adversaries outside the Pale without making further enemies within.

Generally the families of the Pale, for example the Fitzwilliams of Dundrum and Merrion, were loyal to the Crown. In 1559 Thomas Fitzwilliam, who built a castle at Merrion, was returned to parliament as one of the knights of the shire for County Dublin, and in the same year was appointed vice-treasurer of Ireland. In 1566 he received a knighthood from Sir Henry Sidney for his bravery in the field against Shane O'Neill. Furthermore, he was appointed seneschal of the borderlands inhabited by the Walshes, Harolds and Archbolds. Later, Archbishop Loftus of Rathfarnham spoke of him as an eminent man in Ireland.

DALKEY—LIFE WITHIN THE PALE

Dalkey, popularly known as a town though it never had a royal charter, was situated within the Pale, away from the troubles on the frontier. Most of the land at Dalkey was owned by the archbishop of Dublin. Among the tenants who held land here was Johannes de Dalkey, who was admitted to the Dublin Guild of Merchants in 1244–5, suggesting that there was trading here at an early date. In 1284 Richard Talbot held lands at Dalkey directly from the king, for a rent

THE EVOLUTION OF DALKEY CHURCH

The church in Dalkey village is a late medieval building, probably built on the site of an earlier church dedicated to St Begnet. The west end is of thirteenth-century date and may incorporate the north wall of a twelfth-century church. During the fifteenth century, when the village was thriving as a mercantile centre, the church was extended eastwards, and was further modified during the sixteenth century with the insertion of the two-light round-headed window at the east end of the chancel.

Pl. 55—Dalkey church.

of one goshawk a year. Goshawks, hawks used for falconry, were found living wild here along the coast until the end of the eighteenth century. Nine years later Talbot was fined twenty shillings for arrears of rent. In 1326 there were 39 burgesses at Dalkey who rendered the rather high rent of about two shillings per burgage. At about this time John Kendale leased the land at Dalkey from the Priory of the Holy Trinity for an annual rent of three shillings, suit of court and a tax on the ale he brewed. In 1574 Thomas Morgan received land and a garden next to the churchyard for the rent of six shillings and two hens at Christmas, and was required to serve the dean of Christ Church with fish at a reasonable price whenever he was at the grange of Clonkeen.

Dalkey gradually began to prosper after Shankill was effectively abandoned

Province of Leinster.

Engraved by J.Greig from a Drawing by Geo. Petrie for the Excursions through Ireland.

BULLOCK CASTLE,

BULLOCK HARBOUR

This engraved drawing by George Petrie, some time before 1819, shows the harbour at Bullock under the watchful eye of the castle. From an early time there was an important fishing harbour here, and after the dissolution of the monasteries by Henry VIII, when Bullock was confiscated from St Mary's Abbey, the harbour became an important landing dock for passengers *en route* to Dublin.

at the beginning of the fourteenth century. At this time the main economy of the village was fishing. The archbishop's harbour at nearby Colliemore, as well as the harbour at Bullock, were occasionally used as ports, for example when Edward I ordered ships to assemble at Dalkey for the Scottish war in 1302–3. In 1305 Geoffrey de Morton, former mayor of Dublin, and other merchants were arrested for allegedly having sold their cargoes of wine at Dalkey without having paid the tax. However, later in the fourteenth century the mouth of the Liffey became silted up, and docking in Dublin port was precarious. In 1358 the Dublin merchants petitioned the king:

'For want of deep water in the harbour [of Dublin] there never has been

Fig. 26—Bullock Castle, drawn by Petrie.

THE CASTL

Pl. 56a—
Archbold's Castle,
Dalkey.

Tradition has it that there were once seven castles in Dalkey, though today only two survive, Archbold's Castle and Goat's Castle. These were not, in fact, castles but fortified townhouses, built by Dublin merchants who felt it was important to maintain a presence at Dalkey. These merchants were quick to

anchorage for large ships from abroad laden with wine, iron or other commodities. All such anchor at Dalkey within six leagues of Dublin, a town of the archbishop of Dublin. No other place is suitable for laden great ships.'

Soon after, Dalkey harbour became an attractive alternative to Dublin, though it was not an official port. Ships from Britain, France and Spain would

F **DALKEY**

Pl. 56b—Goat's Castle, Dalkey.

use Dalkey as a temporary port, but they also ensured that it did not become a rival to Dublin port itself. Cargoes that arrived at the harbours at Bullock and Colliemore could be stored in these townhouses before being sent to Dublin by horse and cart.

anchor in Dalkey Sound and off-load goods, in particular wine, at Dalkey, from where it could be sent on to Dublin by land, or by smaller crafts along the coast. Often it appears that ships were simply lightened at Dalkey before continuing to Dublin. Carriage to Dublin by horse and cart cost a further two shillings, almost 10% of the cost of the goods.

With the coming and going of ships and goods, Dalkey became prone to smuggling and piracy. In 1313 Peter de Colstoun and Nicholas de Offyngton were charged with robbing a foreign ship at Dalkey and also with the treasonable act of carrying the loot to Robert Bruce in Scotland. As late as 1633 Captain Denny, a notorious pirate, captured a Dutch cargo ship off Dalkey and took the crew captive to the Isle of Man.

Passengers also arrived in Ireland at the port at Dalkey. Among the most distinguished arrivals were John Penros, who arrived as chief justice in 1384, Philip de Courtenay as lord deputy in 1385, Thomas of Lancaster as lord lieutenant in 1402, Sir John Talbot as lord lieutenant in 1414, and Sir Henry Sidney as lord deputy in 1565.

The typically medieval street plan of Dalkey is linear, based on a single street, Castle Street, then known as the Royal Road, with lanes running perpendicularly from it. Only one historical reference survives to a lease in Dalkey, to James Kennan in 1645, whose garden behind the house is specified to be 40 yards long and 13 yards wide. This is quite small, and Kennan paid a high rent of two shillings a year. In 1482 the archbishop was granted the right to hold a weekly market, every Tuesday. This probably took place at the eastern end of Castle Street, where it expands. Furthermore, in that year it was stated that 200 men-at-arms could be mustered to protect the countryside. Even the position of Dalkey within the Pale was no guarantee of security, and the money levied from these markets helped to provide funding for paving of the town, as well as for the construction of the town's defences, traces of which survive south of Castle Street, to the rear of Malrose House and Bayview House. Here the defences consist of an earthen bank rising 2m above the internal ground level, and there was probably originally an outer fosse. There were east and west gates at either end of the main street. Furthermore, several fortified residences were constructed within the town. Tradition holds that there were originally seven castles, but only two of these, Archbold's Castle and Goat's Castle, survive today. Who built these castles and when is not known for certain. They were probably constructed at the end of the fifteenth century, when the provisions were made to defend the town. Rather than being true castles they probably served as the fortified residences of merchants. By the end of the sixteenth century Ringsend was adopted as the port of Dublin; the importance of Dalkey as a port began to decline, and once again fishing became the main economic activity.

THE FINAL CONQUEST

Following the rebellion of Silken Thomas in 1534, Henry VIII decided that the time had come to subjugate the Irish again under the rule of the Crown, and in 1541 he declared himself king of Ireland. However, attempts to prevent the further contraction of the Pale were not immediately successful, and the colony continued to shrink in size until the middle of the sixteenth century. Many of the native Irish and the established Anglo-Norman families felt alienated by the king's dissolution of the monasteries and the ensuing Reformation. Even

RESISTANCE

Right up to the close of the sixteenth century the Irish continued their resistance in the Wicklow Mountains. In 1595 two failed expeditions by Lord Deputy Russell to Glenmalure against the notorious opponent of English rule, Feagh MacHugh O'Byrne, were made from the castles at Bray and Oldcourt. The remaining tower at Oldcourt was originally attached to the east end of a stone-built hall. This hall has since been removed, but the pitch of the gable roof can still be seen in the plaster attached to the west wall of the tower. From the hall access was gained to the tower through a door at first floor level. The Down Survey map of 1657 shows the tower with a conical roof rising above the battlements.

towards the close of the century the Irish of the mountains, under the leadership of Feagh MacHugh O'Byrne, posed a formidable threat to the inhabitants of the Pale. Phelim O'Toole of Powerscourt appears to have remained relatively loyal to the Crown at this time, and served as sheriff of the county of Dublin in 1578. However, his son joined in the rebellion with O'Byrne, and was killed in battle at Glencree in 1582. In 1595 Lord Deputy Russell launched two fruitless expeditions against O'Byrne from the castles at Bray and Oldcourt. In the summer of 1599 a troop of sixty mounted men,

Pl. 57—Oldcourt Castle.

Fig. 27—Killincarrig Castle. Painting by Sam French, 1916 (courtesy of Martin Bernon).

FROM CASTLE TO HOUSE

By the turn of the seventeenth century most of Rathdown had come under English control, and the rebellious O'Tooles and O'Byrnes were restrained in the Wicklow Mountains. Defence no longer dictated architecture, and for the first time the wealthy could afford to construct large houses which were more concerned with providing comforts such as light, heat and space. Henry Walsh of Carrickmines built such a house in Jacobean style at Killincarrig near Delgany. These houses, though still lightly fortified, were the precursors of the large seventeenth- and eighteenth-century mansions, such as at Powerscourt and Kilruddery. Elsewhere earlier tower-houses were simply refurbished, or new buildings were added, as at Monkstown Castle. Unfortunately, the owners of many castles did not accord these buildings the same respect as we might today, and many were demolished in order to provide building material for more modern houses.

THE FORTIFIED HOUSE

Rathfarnham Castle is a fine example of a late sixteenth-century fortified house. It was built as a stately residence by Archbishop Adam Loftus between 1583 and 1585, and largely remodelled by Nicholas Loftus, earl of Ely, during the late eighteenth century. The lines of string-coursing are original and reflect the internal floor levels. Archaeological excavations to the north of the present castle uncovered the remains of an underground vaulted chamber of an earlier castle, perhaps built by the Harold family at the beginning of the fifteenth century.

Pl. 58—
Rathfarnham Castle.

known as the Earl of Southampton's Horse, was stationed at Carrickmines to defend the Pale from the Irish of the mountains. However, they proved to be poor defenders, as the O'Byrnes and O'Tooles devastated and burned the area without opposition.

After an attack by the O'Tooles and O'Byrnes in May 1600 Archbishop Loftus, builder of Rathfarnham Castle, wrote: 'This common calamity hath now light heavily upon myself for even at the writing hereof, the rebels of these mountains by Dublin watching an opportunity to have attempted something against my house at Rathfarnham have not left me so much as one beef or mutton to feed my family'. Clearly the raiding of cattle was still a common tactic of the Irish clans, and other strong castles were prone to such attacks, as is evidenced by a contemporary Gaelic poem:

> *An Fásach Rua, Ráth an Dúin,*
> *Is iad d'argain dob fháth imthnúith;*
> *Fir le crodh cáich do theagar*
> *Fá Ráth Gar do ghluaiseadar.*

> Fassaroe, Rathdown
> the raiding of them was a cause of great envy;
> the men who could collect the cattle from
> all passed by Rathgar.

However, the siege of the Irish around the Pale was unsuccessful because there was no unified cause. In the long run, and particularly in the final years of Queen Elizabeth's rule, the Tudor English were able to take advantage of the disunity that typified the Gaelic clans, and in 1603 the Irish capitulated at the Battle of Kinsale. The old Gaelic way of life ended.

The modern era

In 1609 the Barony of Rathdown was divided in two by the establishment of the county boundary between Dublin and Wicklow. Thomas Fitzwilliam of Merrion was one of the commissioners appointed to determine the limits of the newly constituted County Wicklow. During the seventeenth century, despite internal conflicts, the English monarchy consolidated its rule in Ireland. The Eleven Years' War was a particularly bloody affair, starting in 1641 with the rising of the grandsons of Feagh MacHugh O'Byrne of the Wicklow Mountains. The Catholic gentry of the Pale, such as the Walshes of Carrickmines, also joined the rising. On Saturday 26 March 1641, the Walsh castle at Carrickmines was besieged by a troop of horse and infantry from Dublin, under the command of Sir Simon Harcourt and Lieutenant-Colonel Gibson, who brought reinforcements with two great cannon. The next day a breach was made in the wall of the castle. Apparently all the rebels—men, women and children—were slaughtered, and the walls of the castle were blown up and levelled. The following day Harcourt, who had sustained a bullet wound in the fight, died at Lord Fitzwilliam's castle at Merrion. A poem composed to commemorate his career reflected:

> 'Holland first proved his valour, Scotland stood
> His trembling foe, and Ireland drank his blood'.

During the rising attacks were made on the Protestant clergy and their newly arrived English congregations. Three days after Christmas in 1641, rebels came to the residence of the Rev. Joseph Smithson at Kill and carried off his wife and maid. Both were subsequently hanged by the rebels at Powerscourt. Following an attack on his glebe, the vicar of Rathmichael, the Rev. Simon Swayne, took refuge at Lehaunstown Castle, which was then attacked and set on fire by Robert Barnewall of Shankill and James Goodman of Loughlinstown. Apparently Swayne escaped after being terribly burnt and losing the sight of one eye.

The Irish rebellion and the ensuing Eleven Years' War merged with the Civil War in England, which was fought between Charles I and Parliament, led by Cromwell. The Civil War soon spilled into Ireland with the arrival of Cromwell, and a bloody conflict ensued. An officer in the Parliamentary Army, Lt. Col. Isaac Dobson, who resided at Dundrum Castle, was appointed Commissioner for Revenue and Transplantation for the Civil Survey at the end of the war. He was one of those responsible for the transplantation, under Cromwell's slogan 'To Hell or Connaught', of those landowners who had sympathised with the monarchy.

In 1658 Cromwell died, and two years later Charles II was restored as king.

Pl. 59—Monkstown Castle.

EDMUND LUDLOW AND CROMWELL

One of those dispossessed of his land and exiled to Connacht was Walter Cheevers of Monkstown Castle. His successor at the castle, Lieutenant-General Edmund Ludlow, Cromwell's master of the horse in Ireland, was one of the signatories of the death warrant of Charles I. Ludlow was a staunch republican, but soon after his arrival in 1649 he became disillusioned with Cromwell's tactics in Ireland. In June 1654 Henry Cromwell, son of Oliver, arrived in Ireland. Ludlow entertained him at the castle, showing him his stables and gardens, and expressed concern at his father's violent government. In September 1655 Charles Fleetwood, lord deputy and son-in-law of Oliver Cromwell, stayed with Ludlow at Monkstown before leaving for England. Ludlow became one of the chief opponents of Cromwell's declared Protectorate, and after Cromwell's death he became commander-in-chief of the army in Ireland. After the Restoration of Charles II, Ludlow, because of his anti-Royalist views, was top of the list for execution. He escaped to Switzerland, where he lived in exile under the constant threat of assassination attempts until his death in 1692.

The Parliamentary tenants proved to be only temporary occupants, and the exiles were allowed to return to their homes. In an untypical gesture, the Fitzwilliams allowed the Dobsons to stay at their castle at Dundrum. However, not all lands were returned to their previous owners. John Goodman had been executed for murder some years before, and his castle at Loughlinstown reverted to the Crown. It was granted to Sir William Domville, the attorney-general, in recognition for his work in settling the land claims and disputes arising from the recent war. Walsh of Carrickmines lost out to the earl of Meath, and the Harolds of the Grange to Sir Maurice Eustace.

Towards the end of the seventeenth century the country was once again divided in battle, this time during the war of the kings. Adam Loftus, the grandson of Archbishop Adam Loftus of Rathfarnham Castle, was raised to the peerage by James II but took the side of William III. He was a colonel of a regiment of foot and died at the Siege of Limerick, killed by a cannon ball which was afterwards gilded and hung over the tomb of his family in St Patrick's Cathedral, Dublin. The father of Sir Joshua Allen, who lived at Stillorgan for a time, had come to Dublin from Holland. Prior to the outbreak of the war Joshua moved to Chester, where he came in contact with William III. Perhaps retaining some Dutch sympathies because of his ancestry, he acted as an agent in making arrangements for the embarkation of William's troops to Ireland. His son, Colonel John Allen, served in the army. At the end of the war Joshua returned to Ireland and was appointed first sheriff of Dublin under William III. According to tradition, James II stayed with Sir William Domville at Loughlinstown, and a very ancient tree near the house was planted by the king with his own hands. After the Battle of the Boyne tradition holds that James II slept one night at Puck's Castle and early the next night seized a boat on Killiney strand, sailing to Wicklow, Waterford and on to France. Furthermore, he is said to have stationed two troops of horse at Bray to protect the bridge and to prevent pursuit.

During the comparatively peaceful years of the eighteenth century the populations of south-east Dublin and north-east Wicklow prospered. Many fine mansions were built by the wealthiest landlords in the area, including Rathfarnham House, now Loreto Abbey, built in 1725 for William Palliser, where guests such as Dean Swift, Handel and Thomas Moore were entertained. Powerscourt House near Enniskerry was remodelled *c.* 1731 by the German-born architect Richard Castles. The Domvilles formed an impressive estate at Loughlinstown, and the Fitzwilliams at Mount Merrion. The obelisk at Stillorgan, designed by Edward Lovett Pearse, was built in 1727 as a monument to Lady Allen, who was supposed to be buried there. The obelisk is all that remains of the vast estate of Stillorgan House with its Dutch-style gardens, owned by the Allens, earls of Carysfort.

The gentry thrived during this period, and the hunt became a popular social event in the area, as preserved in the song 'The Kilruddery Hunt', written by Thomas Mozeen. Among the hunters was Johnny Adair from

THE HUNT

An unsigned oil on panel painting known as the Kilruddery Hunt shows the French-style gardens at Kilruddery, commissioned around 1680 by the second earl of Meath and designed by the Versailles-trained Bonet, who had previously been employed by William Petty. The painting shows many features that survive in the gardens today, such as the long twin canals ending at a circular pool enclosed by high hedges of beech and hornbeam, and a lime avenue. A newspaper advertisement of 1711 describes the property as having 'a new Summer House … with 4 rooms on a floor well wainscotted, and in good order, with Pleasure Garden, Cherry Garden, Kitchen Garden, New Garden, Wilderness, Gravel Walks, and a Bowling-Green, all walled about, and well planted with Fruit Trees, with several Canals or Fish Ponds'. The painting shows a plain house, which was refurbished in 1820 when the tenth earl of Meath commissioned the architects William Vitruvius Morrison and his father, Sir Richard Morrison, who lived in Old Connaught. A fine Victorian conservatory was added in 1852.

The painting dates from about 1730, but the figures of the hunt were added some time later in the eighteenth century, probably around the time (*c.* 1744) when Thomas Mozeen celebrated the Kilruddery Hunt in song:

> 'Hark! Hark! Jolly sportsmen, awhile to my tale,
> Which to pay attention I'm sure cannot fail;
> 'Tis of lads and of horses, and dogs that ne'er tire,
> O'er stone walls and hedges, through dale, bog and briar...'

> '...In seventeen hundred and forty four,
> The fifth of December, I think 'twas no more,
> At five in the morning by most of the clocks,
> We rode from Kilruddery in search of a fox...'

Pl. 60—The Kilruddery Hunt.

Kiltiernan, and a place at the Scalp where he narrowly escaped death after following his quarry to the edge of the cliffs is known as Adair's Leap. After a day's chase the huntsmen would frequent Owen Bray's inn, which once stood opposite the gate of Loughlinstown House. Owen Bray was renowned for his necks of mutton and shoulders of venison, as well as for claret and Lisbon. He also provided temporary loans, and was celebrated in song by Mozeen:

'Were you full of complaints from the crown to the toe,
A visit to Owen's will cure you of woe,
A buck of such spirit you never did know,
For let what happen they're always in flow;
'Tis thither the lads of brisk mettle resort,
For there they are sure that they'll never fall short
Of good claret and bullan,
The eighty-fourth bumper for me.'

Fig. 28—Ballybrack dolmen by Gabriel Beranger.

THE EIGHTEENTH-CENTURY ANTIQUARY

Towards the end of the eighteenth century many aristocrats often provided patronage to artists to travel the countryside and make sketches and paintings of antiquities which they could reproduce in their publications. One such artist was Gabriel Beranger, who received patronage from General Charles Vallancey and the Right Hon. William Conyngham. Beranger made many valuable sketches of monuments throughout the country, including several in Rathdown, such as the dolmen in Ballybrack which he painted in 1777. As a note, he wrote: 'it is so much encumbered with all kinds of prickly brambles, that there was no coming near of the supporters to measure them. Even to see them, two of my friends were obliged with their sticks, to keep the brambles down, until I copied their forms.'

STILLORGAN OBELISK

The fine views which could once be gained from Stillorgan Obelisk have been lost, and the fine gardens in which it originally stood have disappeared. The obelisk may have been commissioned by Lord Allen of Stillorgan House as early as 1727, and provided local employment during the famine of that year. It was designed by Edward Lovett Pearce, who also designed the Irish Houses of Parliament (now the Bank of Ireland), and lived his final days in a house on Lord Allen's Stillorgan estate. In 1729 Pearce received Richard Castles as his assistant; only two years later, Castles was commissioned to remodel Powerscourt House. Lord Allen himself was the subject of some of the harshest satires of Dean Swift, who, perhaps unfairly, described him as:

'Positive and overbearing,
Changing still and still adhering,
Spiteful, peevish, rude, untoward,
Fierce in tongue, in heart a coward,
Reputation ever tearing,
Ever dearest friendship swearing,
Judgement weak and passion strong,
Always various, always wrong'.

Pl. 61—Stillorgan Obelisk today.

At the end of the eighteenth century there was a growing interest in Irish antiquities, which became the pastime of many aristocrats and other leading citizens, such as Viscount Jocelyn, lord chancellor of Ireland, who lived at Mount Merrion and provided the antiquarian Walter Harris with funding to publish *Ware's Antiquities* (1764). The Right Hon. William Conyngham of Slane Castle was a patron of the artist Gabriel Beranger, a Dutch Huguenot who made many useful paintings of monuments in south-east Dublin. Thomas Leland, who lived in the rectory at Rathmichael, published *The history of Ireland from the invasion of Henry II* (1773). Joseph Cooper Walker (1761–1810), cousin of the antiquarian Austin Cooper, lived at St Valery, Fassaroe, near Bray. He is perhaps

On one of the surviving architectural drawings for the obelisk Edward Lovett Pearce wrote 'Lady Allen's burying-place, to be a monument to patience'. In fact, Lady Allen died in 1758 and was buried in London, where she had moved after her husband's death. Ironically, beside the obelisk in 1955 the burial of a woman was found (see below and page 27), and excavated by Joseph Raftery. This woman had been buried here in a stone coffin or cist some 3500 years previously.

best known for his published works, which include *Historic memoirs of the Irish bards* (1786) and *An historical essay on the dress of the ancient and modern Irish* (1788). Walker was also elected secretary of the Committee of Antiquities of the Royal Dublin Society soon after its foundation in 1772 by General Charles Vallancey (1725–1812). In 1762 Vallancey purchased land and a lodge house near the avenue gate leading from Blackrock to Mount Merrion, and for a time supervised the construction of a pier at Dun Laoghaire. Vallancey's grandson, Colonel Charles Pratt, an accomplished artist who made many useful sketches of monuments in the area, lived at Rochestown, Killiney.

Another artist, George Victor Du Noyer, was also a celebrated geologist and

Pl. 62—Stillorgan cist under excavation (courtesy of the National Museum of Ireland ©).

THE BOTTLE TOWER

Hall's Barn, also known as the Bottle Tower, near Rathfarnham was erected *c.* 1742 by a Major Hall for storing grain. The tower was modelled on a similar structure known as the Wonderful Barn at Castletown, built around the same time by the Conollys, who had bought the estate and castle of Rathfarnham in 1724.

Pl. 63—Hall's Barn.

antiquary. He was born in 1817 of Huguenot parents, and at the age of seven received art lessons from George Petrie. Both Du Noyer and Petrie made valuable sketches of the monuments in the area. Between 1837 and 1839 Eugene O'Curry and John O'Donovan travelled the countryside of Rathdown on behalf of the Placenames and Antiquities Section of the Ordnance Survey, recording the archaeological monuments and the local traditions associated with them. Many of the monuments they visited have since almost or totally disappeared, and their records preserve a tremendous amount of information that would otherwise have been lost.

Towards the end of the century the Patriot Party under the leadership of Henry Grattan was formed to safeguard the growing wealth and power of the landlords. Grattan, who later lived at Tinnehinch near Enniskerry, sought a 'free Constitution and freedom of trade'. A short-lived parliament, known as

Grattan's Parliament, based in Dublin, was formed in 1782. Fear of invasion resulted in the raising of a Protestant volunteer force to defend the country, and the Rathdown Light Horse headed the procession from the Royal Exchange to the Rotunda during a famous meeting of the Irish Volunteers on 10 November 1783. Led by John Allen, the troopers wore a scarlet uniform faced with black, with white waistcoats, and helmets with red plumes. The Rathdown Volunteers were commanded by Colonel Edwards of Oldcourt, Bray. Fearing a French invasion of Dublin Bay, a military camp (120 acres) was set up at Loughlinstown in 1795, where up to 4000 troops were garrisoned. However, agitation for parliamentary reform and Catholic emancipation became influenced by American and French republicanism, resulting in the 1798 rising of the United Irishmen. There is a tradition that at the Scalp fires were lit to signal the start of the rising. Lord Edward Fitzgerald, who lived at Frescati House near Blackrock, was accused of conspiring with the United Irishmen and establishing contacts with the French revolutionaries. The troops stationed at Loughlinstown played a leading role in quashing the rebellion, and with the ending of the war against the French in 1799 the camp was disbanded.

The Act of Union in 1800 effectively dissolved Grattan's Parliament and brought Ireland into the United Kingdom. In the same year work began on the construction of a military road from Rathfarnham through the Wicklow Mountains, where the rebels of 1798 under the leadership of Michael Dwyer were holding out. The road was guarded by five barracks, including one at Glencree, where another length of road was constructed to Enniskerry. The commanding officer in the mountains, Lt. Col. George Stewart, issued a proclamation on 19 June 1800: 'Notice is hereby given that the mountain roads are now opened by the troops under my command. The possession of those roads, passes and mountains will most effectively open the country, and enable me to protect the persons and property of all its loyal inhabitants . . . and will afford them an opportunity of destroying the banditti that now infest the country; . . . and I will give immediate protection to any of the inhabitants who shall assist me, or any detachment of the troops, in securing any of the gang of Robbers headed by Michael Dwyer.'

A niece of Michael Dwyer, Anne Devlin, was a household servant of Robert Emmet, who leased a house in Butterfield Lane, Rathfarnham, under the assumed name of Robert Ellis, while making preparations for the ill-fated rising of 1803. When he was forced into hiding in the Wicklow Mountains, Anne Devlin became an important contact between Emmet and his comrades in the city, but he was soon captured and brought to trial. Anne was also captured, and although she is said to have been brutally tortured she never revealed the names of her confederates. Emmet's fiancée, Sarah, was the daughter of John Philpot Curran, who lived at The Priory, also near Rathfarnham. Curran was a famous lawyer, but he felt so betrayed by Emmet's rebellion that he refused to defend him at his trial. Baron William Conyngham Plunkett, who resided at Old Connaught House near Bray, though a friend of Wolfe Tone earlier in life,

SOVEREIGN OF THE MOST ILLUSTRIOUS ORDER OF THE LOBSTER

In the late 1780s a humorous, though also serious, satirical society was formed in Dublin's Temple Bar. Its president was elected 'King of Dalkey, Emperor of The Muglins, Prince of the Holy Island of Magee, and Elector of Lambay and Ireland's Eye, Defender of his own Faith and Respecter of all others, and Sovereign of the Most Illustrious Order of the Lobster and Periwinkle'. A coronation ceremony was held on Dalkey Island every summer until 1797. It was discontinued in 1798, such satire being no longer tolerable in the light of the rebellion of that year.

Pl. 64—Dalkey Island.

was chief prosecutor at the trial of Robert Emmet, and William Ridgeway, counsel for the Crown in the trial, lived at Balally. Only a few years earlier Plunkett had strongly supported Grattan in opposing the Act of Union.

In 1821 King George IV visited Dublin as a symbol of the union of Ireland and Britain. Dun Laoghaire was renamed Kingstown in commemoration of his departure from the great harbour constructed there with granite quarried at Dalkey between 1817 and 1821 (the town and harbour were again renamed Dun Laoghaire in 1920). While his yacht was at anchor there he was provided with Wicklow lamb, fruit and vegetables from Leopardstown. On this state visit he stayed at Powerscourt and Kilruddery. In advance of his visit to Powerscourt

MARTELLO TOWERS

In the shadow of constant internal threats, there remained a tremendous fear of the French Emperor Napoleon and the invasion plans he might have for Ireland. Between June 1804 and December 1805, following the renewal of the war between Britain and France, the twelve-mile stretch of coastline from Sandymount to Bray, under the direction of Colonel Benjamin Fisher, was fortified with fourteen Martello towers (based on the Minorcan towers at Adaya, and built at a cost of about £1800 each) and ten artillery batteries, which were generally adjacent to the towers. The towers and batteries were situated so that they all overlapped in their field of fire.

a dam was put in place above the waterfall, and a special viewing platform was constructed near the bottom of the falls. Fortunately for the king he had not enough time to visit the waterfall, for when the dam was removed the ensuing torrent of water swept the viewing platform away. A mountain between Powerscourt and Glencree was named 'Prince William's Seat' in honour of the royal visit.

Counteracting the show of British sovereign power over Ireland was a movement towards Catholic Emancipation led by Daniel O'Connell, who held the first meeting of the Catholic Association at Glencullen House in 1823. The potential rise of Irish nationalism was stalled by the Great Famine, which began

Pl. 65—Silhouette of Dalkey Island Martello tower.

DEFENDING DALKEY ISLAND

The Martello tower on Dalkey Island is the largest of its kind in the area. These towers had a simple arrangement, consisting of three floors: a ground-floor magazine, accommodation for the garrison on the middle floor, and a gun platform on the flat roof (the Dalkey Island tower had two 24-pounder guns). Entrance was generally at first-floor level, reached by a stepladder, through a heavy door covered with iron sheeting on the exterior. Above the door of several of these towers, though not at Dalkey Island, is a machicolation supported on corbels, projecting beyond the parapet, for defence of the door. At the southern end of Dalkey Island, and within musket range of the tower, is a well-preserved battery, with its iron rails and pivots for the traversing platforms.

Pl. 66—Dalkey Island Martello tower.

in 1845. A workhouse was opened at the site of the present Loughlinstown Hospital in 1841 by the Rathdown Board of Guardians in response to poverty and destitution. It is estimated that nearly 1500 people were buried in the 'paupers' graveyard' beside the workhouse during the years before and after the famine, most dying from disease and ill-health rather than from hunger. O'Connell's failure to have the Act of Union repealed led to the founding of the Young Ireland movement, which unsuccessfully attempted a revolution in 1848. One of the leaders of that movement, John Blake Dillon, lived at Druid Lodge, Killiney.

The completion of Dun Laoghaire Harbour in 1821 symbolised the beginning of an industrial revolution in the area, and many of the agricultural lands of the various great estates now became engulfed by industry and housing. This expansion was aided by the construction of the first railway in Ireland, connecting Dublin and Kingstown, which was opened in December 1834 and by 1844 was extended as far as Dalkey. On 10 July 1854 the extension of the railway to Bray was officially opened. Two years later the railway was extended through tunnels in Bray Head to Greystones, under the supervision of Isambard Kingdom Brunel (the famous engineer who designed the Menai Bridge in Wales and the Thames Tunnel in London). Shortly afterwards an inland railway (closed down in 1959) known as the Harcourt Street Line

Pl. 67—Powerscourt House.

DESIGNED ON SHERRY!

Powerscourt House was remodelled *c.* 1731 by the German-born architect Richard Castles. In 1821 King George IV was entertained there. In 1843 Daniel Robertson designed the gardens. Lord Powerscourt wrote of Robertson that 'he was much given to drink and was never able to design or draw so well as when his brain was excited by sherry'. Robertson suffered from gout, and directed work from a wheelbarrow for as long as a bottle of sherry would last. By the time of his death in 1904 the seventh Viscount Powerscourt had transformed the estate.

LEAD-MANUFACTURING

At Ballycorus lead from Glendalough was worked during the nineteenth century, and the highly poisonous fumes were carried by a 1½-mile-long flue to a chimney on the hilltop known as Carrickgolligan. The lead was used for the manufacture of pipes and roofing in the booming building trade as Dublin's suburbs began to expand. Other minerals were also extracted from the flue.

Pl. 68—Ballycorus chimney.

connected Dublin with Rathfarnham, Dundrum, Stillorgan, Foxrock, Carrickmines, Shankill and Bray. By the late 1880s many suburbs, such as Dalkey, became linked by horse-drawn trams to Dublin city centre.

The railways reflect the rise of a Victorian middle class, and their construction encouraged the growth of many fashionable residences throughout the villages and towns of south-east Dublin and north-east Wicklow. The entrepreneur William Dargan initiated the establishment of Bray, nicknamed 'the Brighton of Ireland', as a leisure resort for the middle and upper classes of Dublin city. The town also became a place of fashionable residence, and the prominent surgeon and notable antiquarian Sir William Wilde, father of the colourful and controversial Oscar Wilde, built five high-class residences on Bray seafront. A product of this affluent era was a literary and artistic explosion, and among the suburban participants were George Bernard Shaw, a resident at Torca Cottage on Dalkey Commons, and John Millington Synge, who was born near Rathfarnham and became a pupil at Aravon School in Bray. During the final years of his life Synge lived in Glenageary. James Joyce, who spent his youth in Bray, later taught at a private school called 'Summerfield' on Dalkey Avenue, and lived for a while in the Martello tower at Sandycove. In 1906 the famous playwright Samuel Beckett was born at Cooldrinagh, Foxrock.

In 1879 the National Land League was established to seek agrarian reform, and successfully fought to secure fixed rents for tenants and to prevent landlords from carrying out indiscriminate evictions. The founder of the league was Michael Davitt, who received a gift of the Land League Cottage (now Roselawn) in Ballybrack in recognition of his achievements; he made the cottage his residence from 1888 to 1896. The first president of the Land League was Charles Stuart Parnell. In 1877 the former British prime minister, William Gladstone, visited Ireland, staying as a guest at Powerscourt and Kilruddery, and during his visit he donated £50 for the installation of bells at Christ Church, Bray. In 1886 Parnell convinced Gladstone, recently re-elected prime minister, to seek Home Rule for Ireland. Their campaign failed, and for the next thirty years Irish leaders continued to fight in the British Parliament for Home Rule, but in the meantime others grew impatient.

In 1900, during Queen Victoria's visit to Dublin only a year before her death, no one could foresee the dramatic changes that were to take place over the next century. At this time Éamon de Valera was a boy attending Blackrock College. By 1910, St Enda's (formerly known as The Hermitage) in Rathfarnham had become a school under the tuition of Pádraig and Willie Pearse. In his youth, Roger Casement was a pupil of Aravon School near Bray. Count Horace Plunkett lived at Kiltiernan Abbey, now in ruins, and his son, Joseph Mary Plunkett, became a renowned poet. Eoin MacNeill, a historian, and Bulmer Hobson both lived near Rathfarnham and were co-founders of the Irish Volunteers. Casement, de Valera, Hobson, MacNeill, Plunkett and the Pearse brothers were to become central figures in the formation of Republican and modern Ireland, and during Easter 1916 initiated the most remarkable political changes in this country since the arrival of the Anglo-Normans nearly 750 years earlier.

In archaeological terms a century is a very short time, and although the most recent hundred years have seen changes that have almost totally overshadowed the events of previous thousands of years, we should never underestimate the importance of our past, which has in so many ways shaped our present.

GUIDE TO THE MONUMENTS

Please note that the majority of monuments are located on private land, and the owners may wish to retain their privacy. Arthur Doran (*Bray and environs* (1905)) wrote that

> 'permission to cross the owner's lands is usually freely accorded. Only if you have a mind to meddle with them, remember the fate of the man who for one day's delving into the rath of Calary had half his beard and hair turned white in a single night by the "good people" [the fairies].'

Location of selected monuments

R. Dodder

Rathfarnham

Milltown

Churchtown

Mount Merrion

Edmondstown

Whitechurch

Kilmacud

Dundrum

Stillorgan

Balally

Taylor's Grange

Kilmashogue

Larch Hill

Three Rock Mountain

Ballybrack

Glencullen

Newtown

Ballyedmonduff

Booterstown

Blackrock

Dun Laoghaire

Kill o' the Grange

Monkstown

Kilgobbin

Leopardstown

Stepaside

Jamestown

Ballyogan

Carrickmines

Kiltiernan

Glenamuck

Ballybetagh

Ballycorus

Foxrock

Cornelscourt

Cabinteely

Brennanstown

Tully

Ballybrack

Shanganagh

Loughlinstown R.

Rathmichael

Shankill

Kiltuck

Killiney

Bullock

Dalkey

Dalkey Island

N

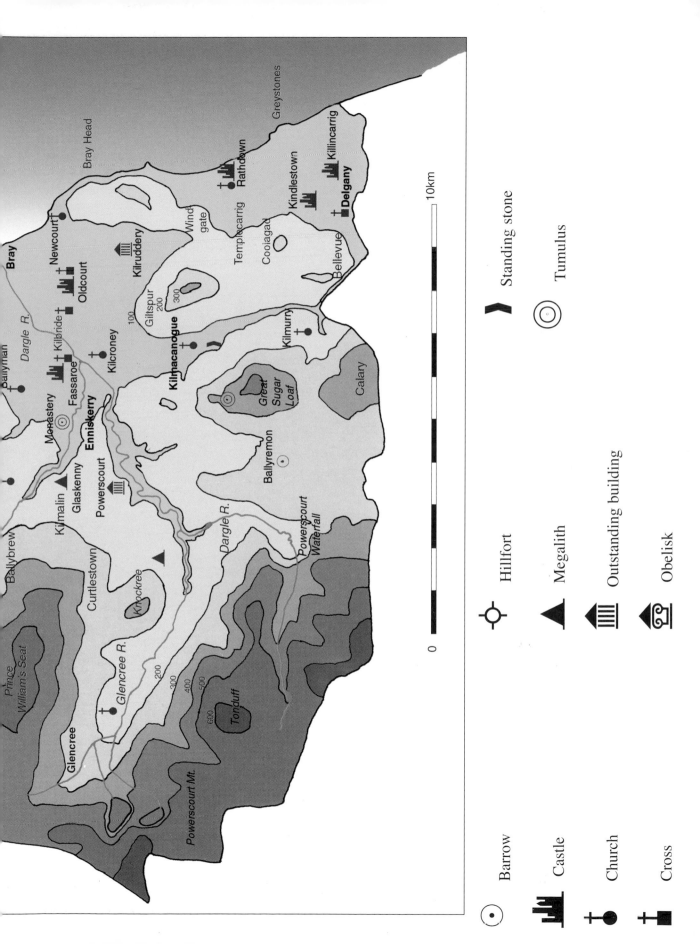

Greystones

Bray Head

Rathdown

Killincarrig

Templecarrig

Kindlestown

Delgany

Coolagad

Bellevue

Wind
gate

Bray

Newcourt

Kilruddery

Giltspur 200

300

Oldcourt

100

Kilbride

Kilmacanogue

Dargle R.

Fassaroe

Kilcroney

Kilmurry

Ballyman

Monastery

Enniskerry

Calary

Great
Sugar
Loaf

Powerscourt

Glaskenny

Kilmalin

Ballybrew

Ballyremon

Curtlestown

Dargle R.

Powerscourt
Waterfall

Knockree

Prince
William's Seat

Glencree

Glencree R.

200

300

400

500

Powerscourt Mt.

600

Tonduff

10km

Standing stone

Tumulus

0

Barrow

Hillfort

Castle

Megalith

Outstanding building

Church

Obelisk

Cross

Megalithic tombs

Ballybetagh

In May 1837 Eugene O'Curry visited a possible cairn known as a Giant's Grave in Ballybetagh, which he described as a cromleac 'about 7ft long and 2 broad and same thickness. It inclines to south resting on the north on the points of a few small stones, about a foot above surface.' This appears to describe the ruined cist or chamber of a burial cairn, which unfortunately has since been destroyed.

Ballybrack (Glencullen)

At Ballybrack near Glencullen is the site of a possible portal tomb recorded in August 1837 by Eugene O'Curry as a Giant's Grave, also known as *Leaba na Saighe*, the 'hound's bed or grave'. The antiquarian Henry O'Neill, who visited the site in 1851, described it as a 'dolmen': 'The roof rock is ten feet long, eight feet broad, and four feet thick, extreme measures; the longest direction of the roof rock is WSW, or nearly E and W. The chamber is greatly disarranged.' The tomb was apparently destroyed in about 1860, and today all that survive are drawings by O'Neill and Du Noyer.

Ballybrack (Shankill)

At Ballybrack near Shankill, above the Loughlinstown River, is a small example of a portal tomb. Presently situated within a residential estate, it bears more resemblance to a modern sculpture than to an ancient memorial tomb. The entrance faces east, and the portal stones are between 1.4m and 1.55m high. The roof stone is 2.2m long, 2.05m wide and 1.2m thick, and the back sits directly on the ground surface.

Ballyedmonduff

At Ballyedmonduff is one of the finest examples of a wedge tomb in the country. In the nineteenth century it was known as a Giant's Grave, and Eugene O'Curry in 1837 said of it: 'I doubt if we have met so perfect a pagan grave in any other counties hitherto examined'. Presently the tomb is situated within a dense pine forest, which has obscured fine views eastwards and southwards, and the Great Sugar Loaf would have formed a very dramatic backdrop to any ceremonies associated with the tomb. The tomb was excavated in 1945 by Seán P. Ó Ríordáin and Ruaidhrí de Valéra.

The tomb consists of a burial gallery, oriented roughly east–west, divided into three chambers. The gallery is surrounded by a stone cairn, delimited by a horseshoe-shaped arrangement of kerbstones (0.5–1m high), with a straight façade at the western end, which also provided a formal entrance to the gallery. The main chamber, situated at the front of the gallery, is divided into two compartments by a miniature sill and jamb arrangement, and was probably roofed by stone corbelling. A closed chamber (1.5m long and 75cm wide) at the rear of the gallery was probably roofed with a capstone. Many of these structural details only became apparent during the excavation of the site.

Within the burial gallery the excavators found over 140 sherds of pottery, representing at least four Beaker vessels, decorated with incised comb and chevron motifs. Only a small amount of cremated human bone was recovered. Also found was a macehead of polished fine-grained stone. It has an hourglass perforation to secure a timber handle, which itself may have been highly decorated. Such artefacts are believed to have been used during social and ritual ceremonies, and were probably an indicator of the owner's status.

Brennanstown

The portal tomb at Brennanstown near Cabinteely, at the bottom of the narrow, steep-sided glen (private residence) beside the Loughlinstown River, is one of the most dramatic prehistoric monuments in Rathdown. The giant capstone of this monument (over 4.5m long and wide, and estimated to weigh over 40 tonnes), resembling the prow of a ship ploughing the stormy seas, rests on two portal stones, 1.5m high, and the entrance faces west. At the rear of the capstone a curious V-shaped groove stretches across the upper surface. The tomb remains unchanged since it was drawn by George Petrie some time before 1819.

Dalkey Commons

A painting by Gabriel Beranger in 1777 is all that remains of a megalith, possibly a passage tomb, known as the Rocking Stone, which once stood at Dalkey Commons. The antiquarian and historian Dalton, who visited the site sometime before 1838, described it as 'a large cromlech of granite, unhewn, but rudely grooved and propped to the usual location', and he went on to say that, despite 'its loneliness, this stubborn witness of antiquity cannot fail to allure the contemplative visitor back to these times . . . amidst all the homage of pagan worship'.

Glaskenny

At the eastern foot of Knockree Hill, high above the Glencree and Dargle river valleys and incorporated within the hedge of the townland boundary of Glaskenny and Onagh, is another impressive example of a portal tomb. The chamber faces north-north-west. One of the portal stones is 3m high; the other is broken and presently stands only 1.8m high. Between the portals is a door stone which stands 2m high; the large roof stone is unfortunately displaced. As one faces the entrance, the Great Sugar Loaf forms an imposing backdrop behind the tomb to the south-south-east. Eugene O'Curry in 1838 recorded the local name of this tomb as *Donnchadh Dearg*. Liam Price suggested that this is a corruption of *dorn a' Deirg*, 'the fist of the Red Giant', but the origins of the name have long been forgotten.

Glensouthwell

At Glensouthwell, Taylor's Grange, is a portal tomb known locally as the Brehon's or Druid's Chair. It is situated on a gentle slope just west of the Little Dargle River. From the site there is a good view northwards over Dublin City. The tall portal stones (2.35m and 2.7m high) and door stone (2.3m high), blocking the original entrance, give the tomb a lanky appearance compared with the short, stout tomb at Ballybrack. The roof stone and back stones are unfortunately missing since at least before 1776, when it was illustrated by Gabriel Beranger, which led Kathleen Turner to speculate that the tomb may have been a modern forgery. However, excavations in the mid-1980s by Valerie Keeley indicate that the tomb is genuine and that it was once surrounded by a roughly circular stone cairn. Cremated bone and charcoal were found in the tomb. A broken quernstone for grinding cereals, sherds of pottery, flint scrapers, blades, knives and a single arrowhead, as well as a large amount of flint waste left over from tool-making, suggest that there was intensive Neolithic settlement in the vicinity of the tomb. Further excavations in 1998 by Rob Lynch have found a hearth, which was sheltered on two sides by windbreaks. Three large pits nearby contained burnt cereal and Beaker pottery, indicating that people were still living here at the beginning of the Bronze Age.

In 1776 Beranger wrote: 'Next and almost close to this Seat, is a cromliach, or Sepulchral monument, supposed to be the Tomb of the Arch Druid, this cromliach's top stone is 8 feet long and being of a spheroidal form I could not determine its breadth and in girth, it stands on 3 supporters from 1 foot to 1 foot six diameter each.' This feature has since disappeared, but may represent the fallen capstone of the dolmen that still stands beside where it once stood.

Pl. 69—Glaskenny dolmen (photograph by Thomas Mason).

Kilmashogue

At Kilmashogue is a wedge tomb, presently located in forestry but no doubt originally situated on an open mountainside overlooking the northern plains, now occupied by Dublin City. The site was excavated by Howard Kilbride-Jones in 1953. The surrounding cairn, originally oval in plan, has been robbed of much of its stone, but has survived relatively intact at the north. Only the sockets of the retaining kerbstones were found. The burial gallery is aligned north-east/south-west. The gap between the two entrance stones at the south-west end of the gallery is only 40cm wide. This was clearly intended to restrict entrance into the gallery, which was divided by a septal stone into two chambers, i.e. a main chamber and a front chamber or portico. Each of the long walls of the chamber was formed by three parallel rows of orthostats set on end. Unfortunately the excavation did not produce any finds associated with the construction and initial use of the tomb, presumably owing to later activity on the site.

Several hundred years later, people returned to the wedge tomb at

Kilmashogue and inserted three stone cists. Cist 1 was a short rectangular grave, 109cm by 61cm by 56cm deep. It contained a Bowl Food Vessel, but no bones were found. The cist had been covered by a circular cairn *c.* 4.5m across. Cist 2 was a short rectangular grave, 56cm by 46cm. It contained the remains of a Bowl Food Vessel and a large amount of cremated bone. The cist was at the centre of a cairn 4.8m across, and along the south there were traces of a retaining kerb of large boulders. Cist 3 was polygonal in plan, consisting of eight upright stones lining a pit dug into the subsoil, with a floor slab; it had been covered by a large slab. The cist was located within the front chamber of the pre-existing wedge tomb, and contained an inverted Enlarged Food Vessel urn and cremated bones.

Kiltiernan Demesne

In Kiltiernan Demesne, marked on the Ordnance Survey maps as a *Cromlech*, is another dramatic portal tomb, situated on a little ledge near the source of the Loughlinstown River valley. The entrance faces north-west. In between the two portal stones (which are 1.25m and 1.4m high) is a door stone, effectively blocking the official entrance into the chamber. The massive, elongate roof stone is 6.5m long, 5.3m wide and 1.55m thick. The chamber was briefly excavated by Marcus Ó hEochaidhe, who found a chert arrowhead, three hollow scrapers and a round-ended scraper. Three rimsherds of coarse pottery were also found. Perhaps these represent grave-goods which accompanied the remains of those buried in the tomb.

The tomb has changed little since it was recorded in a wonderful painting which Gabriel Beranger copied from a drawing made by Vispré in September 1776. Beranger did visit the tomb, for in his painting his comrades, dressed in the gallant costume of the period, take measurements of the tomb, which are provided in an extended commentary. An engraved drawing of the tomb by George Petrie formed the introduction to a volume of his drawings which accompanied Thomas Cromwell's *Excursions through Ireland* (1820).

Larch Hill

At Larch Hill the remains of a portal tomb lie in a picturesque valley beside a bubbling stream. The collapsed chamber faces uphill, and only a tall portal stone (2.5m high) and a side stone still stand. Nearby is the fallen roof stone (3.8m long, 2.65m wide and 70cm thick).

Pl. 70—Larch Hill portal tomb.

Laughanstown

At Laughanstown is a much-disturbed wedge tomb. The site consists of a roughly oval mound or cairn, 14m long (east–west), 12m wide and 1.2m high. The cairn material is largely of local granite and some quartz. Along the north are twelve stones, forming part of a straight-sided kerb 60cm high. The kerb survives only partially along the south, but the overall impression is of a kerb which was originally U-shaped, open at the west. Recent excavations carried out by Christine Grant in 1998 have located extensive prehistoric activity in the immediate vicinity of the tomb.

Parknasilloge

The tomb at Parknasilloge (private residence), near Enniskerry, is presently quite disturbed, but was described by Eugene O'Curry over 150 years ago as a 'perfect unmutilated cromleac' known locally as a Giant's Grave. 'There is first a square enclosure measuring 36 feet in length by 18 feet in breadth. Ten of the large stones which formed this enclosure remain, but those on the S. side have been removed. Immediately within this is a small, circular enclosure, unbroken, and consisting of ten large stones, some laid flat but deep in the ground, others set on edge. In the centre of this circle is the *cromleac*, consisting of an horizontal flag, 5 feet square, and 1 foot 2 ins. thick, supported by three rude stones placed on edge, lengthwise—one on the N., one on the S., and one on the E., each 5 feet long and 2 feet 2 ins. high. The space between the side-stones is 2 feet, and thus a cavity is formed, 5 feet long, 2 feet broad, and 2 feet high. It is open at the W. end, but completely closed at the E. end by the supporters.' From this description and from the remains presently to be seen at the site it could be argued that this represents a disturbed wedge tomb, with a typical entrance opening to the west, and enclosed by a circular kerb.

Shankill

During the construction of the Carrickmines–Bray Gas Pipeline in 1998, John O'Neill found and excavated a previously unrecorded wedge tomb overlooking the modern village of Shankill. The tomb appears to have been built on top of a *fulacht fiadh*. To the north of the trough of the *fulacht* was a cobbled area surrounded by an arc of post-holes, probably originally supporting a timber windbreak. North of this were found the stake-holes of a small, oval hut site. Sometime later this *fulacht* fell out of use, and a wedge tomb was built on the site. The tomb consisted of a double-walled gallery 2.4m long (east–west), 1.5m wide at the west end and 3.4m across at the east end, which was the entrance to the tomb. No roof stones survived and no evidence for a burial was found, suggesting that the tomb had been badly damaged. Sometime later it was covered under material dug by people in search of a spring well, in which was placed a trough of another *fulacht fiadh*. Ploughing in recent years had turned up much of the burnt stone and charcoal of this *fulacht*, and the landowner had always called this area the 'black corner of the long field'. Following the excavation in 1998 the tomb was reburied.

Only a few stones survive of a megalithic tomb in an area of Shankill known locally as 'Carrig-gollane'. The tomb is presently overgrown, but otherwise has changed little since the early nineteenth century, when it was drawn by Du

Noyer. An engraved drawing by Petrie sometime before 1819 appears to show the tomb more complete. One support stone is only 0.92m high, whereas the other is 1.53m high, giving the 2.3m-long roof stone an unusual tilted, almost drunken, appearance. The site has a fine view southwards towards the two Sugar Loaf mountains.

Pl. 71—Megalithic tomb at Parknasilloge (photograph by Thomas Mason).

Two Rock Mountain

The passage tomb on the summit of Two Rock Mountain, known as Fairy Castle, consists of a roughly circular turf- and heather-covered stone cairn (25m across and 2m high) of granite and occasional quartz blocks. On the summit of the cairn are an early Ordnance Survey cairn and a replacement trigonometrical point. Owing to collapse of the edges of the cairn, the entrance is presently invisible. Near the centre of the cairn is presumably a small burial chamber.

Rock art

Onagh

In a field in Onagh is an isolated outcrop of rock, from which there is a very fine view of the Great Sugar Loaf. The rock, only 45cm high, has been severely weathered, but it still retains traces of a large circular depression, 20cm across and 8cm deep, and at least five small cupmarks (averaging 4–5cm across). According to local tradition, fairies were once seen around this stone.

Ballyedmonduff

Pl. 72—Monastery tumulus.

Lying loose on the southern side of the cairn of the Ballyedmonduff wedge tomb is a granite block (70cm long, 40cm wide and 20cm thick), on one surface of which are seven cupmarks.

Cairns and tumuli

Ballybrew

In a field in Ballybrew lies a circular cairn, 21m across and 0.9–1.4m high, consisting of loose stones, with some possible kerbstones at the north and south-west.

Glencap Commons

Two small cairns, probably covering Early Bronze Age burials, are located in Glencap Commons on the northern shoulder of the Great Sugar Loaf, with a commanding view over Powerscourt, the Scalp, Killiney and Dalkey. The northern cairn is the larger of the two (11.5m in diameter and 1.2m high) and was disturbed during unsuccessful excavations by Liam Price in 1933. It is clear that their siting was carefully chosen, not only because of their impressive view over so much territory, but also because they can be seen from ground level, particularly from the main Dublin–Rosslare road as one enters the village of Kilmacanogue.

Killiney

At Killiney was a tumulus described by King, writing in 1799, as an earthen mound 41m in diameter, enclosed along its circumference by a stone circle or kerb, and there may have been a surrounding ditch. The mound was apparently opened in 1787, and skeletons and urns of baked clay were discovered in stone coffins. The tumulus was situated at the 'Druid's Judgement Seat', which Wakeman in 1892 suggested was a modern antique or folly, made from the ruins of this tumulus.

Monastery

At Monastery near Enniskerry is a high oval mound (17.5m west-north-west/east-south-east, 12.5m north-north-east/south-south-west, and 5m high) with a flat top 5m in diameter. The mound is covered in trees and the sides are quite eroded. From the top of the mound there is a commanding 360° view, dominated by the two Sugar Loaf mountains to the south and the Scalp to the north. Eugene O'Curry, who visited the site in 1838, said that it was locally called a Fairy Moate, and he believed that it was originally enclosed by a ditch and outer bank at the base, though no trace of these survives today. On the border of Monastery, in Fassaroe, a polygonal cist containing the cremated bones of an adult male was found in a field known locally as the 'Moat field', suggesting that a burial mound formerly stood here also.

Powerscourt

In an edition of *Ware's Antiquities* translated and edited by Harris in 1764 there is a description of a find made in the vicinity of Powerscourt. Ware referred to sepulchral mounds of stone and earth, which he called 'mounts', and very briefly described the discovery in one mound of six urns; one that he illustrated resembles a Bowl Food Vessel. Describing this vessel, he claimed that 'the capacity of it, if entire, would not much exceed a Quart; it is of light brown Colour, and composed of a crumbling soft Clay, rudely enough wrought, and each Urn was covered with a small flat stone, and filled with black Dirt, which possibly might be the Ashes reduced to that Condition by Time'.

Unmarked prehistoric burials

Ballybrew

At Ballybrew, between Enniskerry and Glencullen, a small flat cemetery of three cist graves was found during the course of gravel-digging. Cist 1 was rectangular in plan (92cm long, 61cm wide and 61cm deep) and had a paved floor. Within the grave was the crouched skeleton of a young adult female. A Bowl Food Vessel (the mouth of which was apparently covered with a stone) stood opposite the face of the deceased. A broken lignite bead was found near the left hand, and a small flint scraper near the knees. It appears that the body may have been placed on a rush matting. Cist 2 was also rectangular in plan (112cm long and 76cm wide) and contained the crouched skeleton of a young adult male, lying on its back, head to the east. A Bowl Food Vessel stood near the skull and contained two unburnt bone fragments of another skeleton which was scattered to the north of Cist 2. A third cist was also excavated, but was apparently filled with earth and had been disturbed.

Ballyman

The files of the National Museum of Ireland record two pit burials at Ballyman which contained cremation burials within Enlarged Food Vessel Urns. One of the cremations was of a young adult male, whose bones were crushed before being placed in the urn. The other urn contained the remains of an adult and a juvenile, though the genders of the individuals could not be identified. In both cases the individuals had been well cremated, but the burials were incomplete and it appears that not all of the cremated remains were collected before being placed in the urns. The burials were radiocarbon-dated by the National Museum of Ireland to about 1370 BC.

Cabinteely

A small urn in a stone cist was found in 1857 at Cabinteely. No other information is available.

Calary Lower

At Calary Lower an inverted Encrusted Urn containing the cremated remains of a child was found in a polygonal cist.

Dalkey Island

Excavations on Dalkey Island uncovered a small number of probable Early Bronze Age burials. One consisted of the skeleton of an adult male dated to about 2300 BC. The skull contained about 50 periwinkle shells. Three other burials found are probably also of Early Bronze Age date, including the crouched skeleton of an adult male, and two skeletons lying face down, with the hips twisted around laterally so that the thighs could extend out sideways with the calves drawn tightly back behind them and the feet behind the buttocks.

Deansgrange

At Deansgrange a short, rectangular, slab-built cist (63cm long, 40cm wide and 44cm deep) was found, covered by a capstone. It contained fragments of the skeletons of two adult individuals. One was a male, but it was not possible to identify the gender of the other.

Edmondstown

At Edmondstown an extensive cemetery was discovered in December 1950 and subsequently excavated by P. J. Hartnett. A total of 27 individuals were found within several pits and cists. One individual had possibly been trepanned. Thirteen burials were accompanied by pottery vessels. Cist I was a rectangular stone-lined grave (1.3m long and 1m wide) of granite slabs covered by a capstone, and contained a crouched skeletal burial of a young adult, accompanied by a Bowl Food Vessel. Pit 5 consisted of a simple pit measuring 48cm by 30cm and contained an inverted Encrusted Urn (33cm high), decorated with an applied chevron band with bosses in the angles. The urn contained a large quantity of cremated bone, representing four individuals—

one adult, two children (5–12 years of age) and one infant. Within Pit 11 was a Collared Urn containing the cremated remains of three individuals.

Jamestown

At Jamestown, near Stepaside, a flat cemetery representing at least three burials was found during sand-quarrying operations since 1908. An Encrusted Urn was reported from the site, but no details of the discovery survive. A Vase Food Vessel was 'found in a cist covered by a flat granite slab about 6ft square, the walls 2ft deep, and built of loose rubble granite, the floor being flagged with granite slabs. The Urn was in the centre of the cist, the floor of which was strewn with human bones', which had been cremated. In 1927 a Bowl Food Vessel was found in a cist with a capstone and paved floor, along with unburnt human bones.

Kilmacanogue

In a sand-pit at Kilmacanogue a small cist was found which contained a pygmy cup and cremated bone.

Stillorgan

On 26 June 1716 a stone-built cist, 61cm long, 38cm wide and 36cm deep, was found by workmen digging a tunnel through a hill leading to the gardens south of the old Stillorgan House. The find was investigated by the Dublin antiquarian Thomas Molyneaux, who claimed that the cist grave had been covered by 'one huge massy stone, that ten men could not lift, which lay about two feet beneath the surface of the ground'. On removal of this stone, 'which was done with no small difficulty', they discovered the skeletal remains of an adult male. According to Molyneaux, 'these lay promiscuously dispersed, within the hollow of the grave, and by them stood the urn, containing none of the fragments of the bones, nor anything else'. Molyneaux was fascinated by the fact that these bones were incomplete and so scattered within the grave, and remarked that they had not been cremated before burial. He concluded that the body had never been burnt 'but that it had lain buried in another place for some time past, and the loose bones, afterwards collected hence, were here deposited within the compass of this narrow grave; yet to retain some of the ancient fashion of the country, which men don't easily quit all at once, 'twas thought a decency and a respect due to the deceased, to inter an urn together with the bones, tho' it was not apply'd as usual, for the reception of the ashes of the dead'. A surviving drawing of this pot suggests that it was a Bowl Food

Vessel, i.e. a grave-good rather than a true urn.

Beside the obelisk at Stillorgan Park a disturbed cist was discovered in 1955; it contained the disturbed remains of the skeleton of an adult female, whose death was due to a (sacrificial?) blow to the skull.

Ticknock

A cremation contained within an inverted Enlarged Food Vessel Urn was found in a simple pit at Ticknock.

Fulachta fiadh

Ballyremon Commons

On Ballyremon Commons, west of the Great Sugar Loaf, a group of at least four *fulachta fiadh* were discovered a number of years ago by Paddy Healy on the margins of an island in the blanket bog. A typical example is horseshoe-shaped, 9m across and 45cm high. One was excavated by Victor Buckley, who found a clay-lined oval pit (2m long, 70cm wide and 40cm deep), surrounded by three stake-holes; these may represent a timber tripod which hung over the water-filled pit in which the food, possibly joints of meat, was boiled. The charcoal from one of these stake-holes produced a radiocarbon date of around 1400 BC. Surrounding the pit was a circular concentration (9m across) of the heat-cracked granite stones which had been used to heat the water.

Killincarrig

At Killincarrig near Delgany a *fulacht fiadh* was excavated and found to consist of an extensive spread of burnt stone, 24.5m by 15m. The excavator, Alan Hayden, uncovered a subcircular clay-lined trough, 1.9m in diameter and 90cm deep. The site was radiocarbon-dated to around 1600 BC.

Standing stones

Cabinteely

In a modern housing estate is a roughly squared granite standing stone, 1.38m high. It was excavated by Judith Carroll in advance of the construction of houses. It was found to have been inserted in a small pit and to be supported by small packing-stones. A few fragments of cremated human bone were found

Pl. 73—A local farmer (Peter O'Neill) at the Glencullen standing stone (courtesy of John Scarry, Dúchas—The Heritage Service).

nearby, suggesting that the stone was erected as a burial-marker. The stone was then moved and re-erected in its present position, a short distance from where it originally stood.

Glencullen

At Glencullen is a large, impressive, quartz standing stone, 1.83m high by 92cm wide, roughly squared. Today the stone is known as Queen Mab, but when Eugene O'Curry visited it in 1837 he was informed locally that it had no name; the name 'Queen Mab's stone' may have been attached to it more recently. Kathleen Turner recorded an old local story of an unsuccessful attempt to find the base of the stone, despite digging to a depth equivalent to its height. Apparently there was once another quartz standing stone near the old church in the village.

Kilmurry

In Kilmurry near Kilmacanoguc is a stone, 1.7m high, 65cm wide and 30cm thick, impressively situated in the shadow of the Great Sugar Loaf.

Kilmashogue

In a field beside the road from Marlay Park to Rockbrook are two standing stones. One is a tall granite pillar, 2.05m high, roughly squared (41cm wide and 38cm thick). Approximately 68m west-north-west stands a second granite pillar, presently leaning slightly to the north. It would originally have stood 1.83m high. From this site there is a commanding view northwards over Dublin City.

Pl. 74—Kilmurry standing stone.

Ring-barrows

Ballyremon Commons

The ring-barrow at Ballyremon Commons is situated on high ground in the foreground of the Great Sugar Loaf. It consists of a circular mound 12m in diameter and 1.5m high, surrounded by a ditch 2.5–5m wide and 1m deep, with traces of an outer bank 2.5–4m wide and 20–95cm high. The site has been truncated on the north side by a field boundary.

Newtown

On top of the hill at Newtown, above the village of Glencullen, is a grass-covered ring-barrow with a standing stone nearby. The site has a panoramic view southwards towards the two Sugar Loaf mountains. The mound, which has been disturbed by the digging of rabbits rather than antiquarians, is 16.5m in diameter and 1.2m high. A shallow ditch (2.2m wide at the base and 40cm deep) encloses the mound. A granite standing stone (1.6m high) is situated immediately to the east-north-east of the ring-barrow. Some distance to the east was a heap of earth and stones, described by Eugene O'Curry in May 1837, which was known locally as 'Ossian's Grave'.

Hillfort

Rathmichael

On the wooded hilltop of Rathmichael, overlooking Shankill, are the poorly preserved remains of a hillfort. The entire summit of the hilltop (about 120m in diameter), specially chosen for its large yet compact and defensible area, was originally enclosed by an impressive earth and stone bank and a deep outer ditch, which has since been reduced to a low embankment 30cm high—a poor reflection of the original ramparts. There is a splendid view from the site, northwards over Dublin City (then rolling agricultural land), eastwards towards Killiney and Dalkey, and southwards towards the two Sugar Loaf mountains. This must have been an important defended settlement in its day, and indicates a political centre of a wealthy chieftain of some kind in south-east Dublin.

Churches and other ecclesiastical remains

Balally

At Balally in south Dublin are the foundations of a church (12.4m east–west by 7.2m north–south). The walls of undressed, mortared granite boulders only survive to a height of 45cm. The earliest known historical reference to the site is in the late thirteenth century, but there are indications that this was once the site of an important Early Christian monastic foundation. Aerial photographs reveal that the site was enclosed by a substantial oval earthen bank, enclosing an area 148m across, with traces of an outer enclosure at the southern edge of the site. Excavations in 1990 by Charles Mount found two sheet-bronze fragments, which formed the upper and lower plates of a strap-tag. The upper plate is decorated with a simple incised interlaced design, typical of Early Christian art. The placename Balally (*baile Amhlaibh*, 'the town of Óláf') may commemorate a Viking saint.

Ballyman

At the bottom of the picturesque River Dargle valley are the ivy- and bramble-covered remains of Ballyman church, of which only the east gable and a portion of the south long wall are still upstanding. A cashel wall enclosed the site until 1850. In the east gable of the church is a fine example of a round-headed window, probably of early thirteenth-century date. A window in the south wall has collapsed and was originally spanned by a reused Rathdown slab. This is a large slab decorated with a central band on which are two cupmarks, each enclosed by four concentric circles. The rest of the slab is filled in with a herringbone design. A fragment of a second Rathdown slab was used as the side stone of the ambry in the east wall.

Before 1216 the site belonged to Glendalough, and this link is emphasised by the dedication of the church to St Sillán, who was an early bishop at Glendalough. Near the church was a holy well dedicated to St Kevin, the founder saint of Glendalough. The well was still used at the beginning of the nineteenth century, and was surrounded by trees on which rags were tied by pilgrims. Excavations by Elizabeth O'Brien in the vicinity of the church revealed a corn-drying kiln, radiocarbon-dated to around AD 425. It is not clear if this kiln was associated with a very early ecclesiastical foundation at the site. These excavations also produced a fine fragment of a penannular brooch with zoomorphic terminal, dated to between the sixth and seventh centuries. The terminal was decorated with a square millefiori setting, a rayed design (red on yellow) representing rounded eyes, and an upturned snout with medial ridge. The pin head is decorated with an incised saltire.

Excavations at Ballyman also revealed thirteenth- and early fourteenth-century metal production on the site, at a time when the church was in the possession of the Knights Templar. Later the church was granted to the Priory of St John of Jerusalem, and was occasionally called 'Mouncton' (Monkstown/town of the monks) at this time. This metal production site was represented by a cobbled area associated with thirteenth-century pottery known as Leinster Ware and an iron lobe-headed pin. A large amount of slag and furnace bottoms were also found, though there was no clear evidence for what was being manufactured at the site. In 1336 one of the Harold family was accused of stealing timber from the house of the prior here.

In 1838 D'Alton wrote that St Kevin's Well was 'overshadowed by an ash tree, thickly entwined with ivy; and interlaced with such pendant scraps of cloth and linen, as a strange and inveterate superstition, singularly coinciding with a custom in the land of their eastern fathers, induces the Irish peasantry to fling over those stations of their reverence and prayer'. Near it, he wrote, 'in the midst of hawthorn trees, are the ruins of an old church, twelve feet long by seven wide, having but one solitary grave beside it — a large monumental stone — uncarved — unlettered — in an awful solitude — smothered by thorns and nettles — unsuggested by the pathway of devotion or affection. — It is the grave of a suicide!'

Blackrock

In the village of Blackrock is a Fassaroe-type cross, probably moved here from some unrecorded church site in the locality. The small granite cross is finely shaped, with chamfered edges. It is unusual in that it bears no Crucifixion scene; instead there is a head carved in high relief, and on the opposite face is a curious abstract incised pattern.

In 1865 a proposal by the Town Commissioners to have the cross replaced sparked off a controversy. At that time a certain Captain Sheffield Betham gave the following account of the history of the cross:

'In the reign of Queen Elizabeth, Sir John Travers, a man of note, lived in Monkstown Castle. He had an only daughter, who had a son, drowned on Merrion Strand, and two daughters. One of those daughters was married to Byrne of Cabinteely, and the other to the ancestor of Lords Longford and De Vesci. The estate was divided—the Byrnes getting the portion called Newtown-on-the-Strand, or Newtown-Castle-Byrne. The Cross was the property of the Byrne family, and was always repaired by them, and was a landmark of the boundary of the city jurisdiction—the line coming down the lane at Old Merrion Churchyard, and running along the centre of the road as far as the Cross of Blackrock; thence in a straight line to the sea where the old Bath-street used to run, extending out to the sea as far as a man could wade at low water and cast a javelin. The cross is not, and never was, an ecclesiastical one, but simply a boundary, and the city people, when they rode the "fringes", came up to it as their extreme limit.'

*Pl. 75—
Blackrock Cross.*

The claim that this was not an ecclesiastical cross is probably untrue. Perhaps it belonged to a lost church in the locality, or perhaps at one time it marked the boundaries between churches. Certainly the cross acted in more recent times as a boundary-marker between the city and the county, and the ritual described above, used by the lord mayor of Dublin to reinforce the claims of the city to the outlying lands, may have originated in the fifteenth century. At the beginning of the twentieth century, funeral processions to the local church carried coffins in a circle in front of the cross. This done, the men would face the cross and a few prayers were said.

Cabinteely

In 1998 Malachy Conway excavated the remains of an extensive cemetery prior to the construction of an Esso filling station near Cabinteely village. The site was located on a natural knoll known as Grave's Moat, after a local landowner. According to local tradition Grave ploughed the land, and overnight his hair turned white for causing the cemetery to be disturbed. The recent excavations revealed over 1550 burials, placed in graves simply cut into the earth, though some had been lined with timber or stone. The cemetery had been in use from the fifth century and fell out of use in the twelfth century. In some cases stones had been placed beside or under the heads of those buried. Many small pins were found, indicating that the burials had been shrouded. Other finds included stick- and ring-pins, knives, buckles, shears, gouges, bone and glass beads, bone handles and combs. A variety of pottery was also found, much of which had been imported from France. The cemetery was enclosed by three ditches, which may have been sequential. There was no direct evidence for a church, which may have been abandoned long before the cemetery fell out of use. The site is probably that from which the local name Kilbogget derived (perhaps a corruption of *Cill Beccan*).

Carrickmines

In Carrickmines, on a private farm, is a socket in an earthfast boulder which represents the base of a cross. It is situated one mile from the church sites of Tully to the east and Jamestown to the west, and may have marked a route or boundary between the two.

Dalkey

In Dalkey village is the site of a church dedicated to St Begnet. The present church in Dalkey village is almost entirely later medieval. However, the east end of the north wall of the nave does appear to be of different masonry, consisting of larger granite blocks than used elsewhere in the church, and may represent an early medieval building incorporated within the later building. In this section of wall there is also a round-headed window, which may be the original east window of the earlier twelfth-century church subsequently inserted into the north wall. Above this window, externally, is a stone with faint traces of a small Latin cross with splayed terminals.

The church ruins largely consist of a substantial thirteenth-century nave (14.5m east–west by 5.1m north–south) and a later chancel. The nave features a pointed-arched door in the south wall and a nearby holy water stoup and trefoil-headed inset, also in the south wall.

At the south-west end of the nave there is a low, narrow doorway (1.25m high and 65cm wide on the inside). This doorway, despite its size, is fascinating as it has bar holes on the outside, indicating that the timber door could only be locked from the outside. This would make no sense unless there was a structure outside the west gable. On the outside of this wall, three levels of stone teeth projecting from either side of the gable would have acted as a brace to secure such a building, and a rebate above the level of the door could have carried the support beams of a timber floor. This indicates that it was intended to construct a building, probably a residence or a bell-tower, on the outside of the west gable of the nave, and that this was an integral part of the nave design. However, there is no record of a building here, and the large, thirteenth-century Gothic sandstone window in the west gable may indicate that the project was never carried out.

It is difficult to date the construction of the chancel (7.9m long) and the insertion of the elegant chancel arch (3.6m wide and 2.55m high). The two-light round-headed window with a hood-moulding at the east end of the chancel is typical of the sixteenth century. It is not clear if this is a later insertion or if it dates the actual construction of the chancel.

In the surrounding graveyard are further reminders of the antiquity of this church site. Situated just outside the north wall of the church is a Tau cross only 45cm high. Also from the graveyard are two Rathdown slabs. Now located in the nearby heritage centre is a large heavy slab bearing a ringed Latin cross with sunken quadrants and a cupmark at the intersection. Below the cross is a cupmark enclosed by a large circle, and at either end of the slab is a cupmark enclosed by two concentric circles, the lower example of which is broken across. According to tradition, in 1855 a Dalkey pilot named Red Bill Harford, at the age of 101, brought some friends to the graveyard and pointed out to them the spot where he desired to be buried. When digging his grave shortly afterwards they came upon this slab. Perhaps Red Bill knew of a holy stone buried here and chose this spot as his own burial-place. The fragment of a second Rathdown slab was found near the northern boundary wall of the graveyard. The weathered decoration consists of a cupmark and a herringbone pattern.

In the graveyard were found two fragments of an Early Christian type of rotary quern (original diameter 44cm). The pieces, of granite, appear to represent the upper grinding stone of a quern which originally had an hourglass-shaped perforation to allow the grain to pass through onto the basal stone. A cross-inscribed grave-slab with an outline Latin cross, probably removed from the graveyard, was reused in the fifteenth century as a door lintel at the nearby Archbold's Castle.

In November 1807 two troop ships (the *Prince of Wales* and the *Rochdale*) were wrecked in Dublin Bay, with the loss of about 380 lives. Little over half the bodies were recovered, and many were buried in the graveyard here and at Monkstown. The sinking of these ships fuelled arguments for the construction of the Asylum Harbour at Dun Laoghaire, on which work began ten years later.

Dalkey Island

Early Christian hermitages are traditionally associated with the many islands along our western Atlantic seaboard. The church, dedicated to the female St Begnet, on Dalkey Island off the Dublin coast may have been founded as just such a hermitage. St Begnet supposedly belonged to the Dál Messin Corb, the rulers of the territory at the dawn of history. The island is mentioned in the annals in 727, when a cow was seen with one head, one body, two hind parts, two tails and six legs, and gave milk three times a day.

The present stone church on the island (internal dimensions 7.5m east–west by 5m north–south), featuring antae and a flat-lintelled west doorway, represents a classic example of an eleventh-century Irish church. Later the church was modified, with the addition of a late medieval belfry on the west gable. Archaeological excavation on Dalkey Island uncovered a number of roof slates and glazed ridge tiles belonging to the Anglo-Norman roofing of the Early Christian church. Also found was a window fragment of Dundry stone, part of the east window which was inserted into the pre-existing church in the thirteenth century and which in turn was dismantled during the construction of a nineteenth-century brick fireplace. Dundry stone was specially imported by the Anglo-Normans from near Bristol for use at Irish church sites. At this time the church was assigned to the Priory of the Holy Trinity in Dublin.

Liversage's excavations also found that the church was enclosed by a rubble stone and earth wall, defined internally and externally by stone slabs set on their sides. During the excavation a post-hole was found which would have held a timber post to support a gate. The original height of the wall was less than 90cm, indicating that this enclosure was not intended to be defensive or to keep out stock but was probably constructed to define the consecrated ground around the church. Outside the church the excavator found part of a cemetery. Eleven burials were found, and three of the deepest may be associated with the earliest use of the church. Both female and male adults were represented, as well as two children, indicating that this was not simply an ecclesiastical cemetery.

There are two large incised crosses on the vertical faces of rock outcrop opposite the church. One is a ring-headed cross with slightly splayed arms enclosed in a circle, perhaps dating from the eighth century. The other is a similar ring-headed cross with slightly splayed arms, and with small bosses at the intersection of the arms where they pass through the ring.

Delgany

In the picturesque village of Delgany in Wickow is a church site dedicated to St Chuaróg or Mochorog, who was of royal Welsh descent and who apparently gave the last rites to St Kevin of Glendalough when he died in 618. It is a disappointment that all that survives of the church is an undressed, roughly coursed portion of the north long wall (72cm thick and 1.5m high), which has traces of plaster. These remains appear to be of a post-medieval church which continued in use until 1789. The rest of the church walls have been reduced to grass-covered foundations, and it appears that the building originally measured 26m east–west by 6m north–south. The surrounding graveyard is full of eighteenth- and nineteenth-century headstones. The only archaeological evidence for an early ecclesiastical foundation at the site is represented by a granite shaft, 1.8m high, of a high cross. On the south face is an inscription which reads:

> OR DO
> ....
> OCUS
> DO O
> DRAN
> SAIR

('A prayer for .... and for Odran the wright'). The inscription asks for a prayer for two people. Unfortunately the first name is illegible. The second person named, Odran, was a wright (someone working with wood), but the name cannot be identified with certainty in the historical sources. However, the naming of a woodworker on a cross may indicate that Odran's trade was specifically associated with the church; perhaps he was a builder of wooden churches or a carver of wooden crosses. The name Odrain is preserved in the name of an unlocated church, Baliuodrain, mentioned in the *Crede Mihi* as lying in the territory between Bray and Delgany.

Fassaroe

At Fassaroe the twelfth-century granite cross, 1.4m high, has four weathered carved heads, one representing a bishop wearing a mitre. The cross is sometimes called St Valery's, after the name of the nearby house. According to Anne Plumptre, who stayed with the Walker family of St Valery in 1814 and 1815, the cross 'was brought from a glen at some distance, and stood originally in the centre of the little paddock, round which runs the plantation. But it became so much an object of devotion among the neighbourhood, that paths without number were made over the grass to get to it.' This suggests that the cross was moved, possibly from Ballyman, to its present position, where it was more accessible to pilgrims.

However, there are reasons to believe that the cross was moved to Fassaroe because there was a church ruin here, and when Eugene O'Curry visited here in December 1838 he saw a font and a cross shaft, and reported that a quern and a font had been removed to the house adjacent to the nearby castle. Furthermore, he was informed that human bones had been dug up on the south side of the cross. Francis E. Ball claimed in 1900 that someone he knew remembered traces of a building in an adjoining field, believed to be the remains of a church.

Jamestown

The name Jamestown was given to the townland during the early years of the Reformation. This area once formed part of Ballyogan, then known as Ballemochain, preserving the name of a foundation dedicated to St Mochaime (d. 584), a brother of St Kevin of Glendalough. Presently there is no trace of this church, but its site is marked by a well and a nearby granite cross, 1.5m high. One face has a crudely carved figure in relief, perhaps a sheela-na-gig. The arms of the hunch-backed figure appear to spring from behind the ears, the hands are collapsed in front of the body, and the legs hang from the hips, with feet pointed outwards. On the opposite face of the cross the carving consists of a raised ring, apparently an outline of a head, from which raised lines extend vertically down the shaft. Curiously, the bottom of the shaft has a tenon, but no base exists at this site and the cross has been inserted directly into the ground.

Killarney

Nothing now remains of the church of Killarney (known in Irish as *cill easpuig Sáráin*, 'the church of Bishop Saran'), presently (and mistakenly) located in the townland of Kilbride, on the outskirts of Bray. In 1837 Eugene O'Curry described the foundations of a building about 9m east–west by 3.5m north–south, and noted a possible enclosing bank. He was told that fairies and ringing bells were often heard about it. Today the site is marked by an upright granite slab, 1.22m high, with a Greek cross carved in relief, and a domed boss below each arm. At the end of the twelfth century Walter de Ridelesford granted the church to his priory of Graney in Kildare.

Kilbride

At Violet Hill, on the outskirts of Bray, an Early Christian cemetery was disturbed around 1885 during the construction of a dam. The cemetery was situated on the flattened surface of a knoll surrounded on three sides by a stream. Unfortunately, the site was not scientifically excavated. It is recorded that a rectangular area (6m east–west by 5.5m north–south) was enclosed by a drystone wall with a foundation of large boulders and an entrance at the east. Within the enclosure two Rathdown-type grave-slabs were found, oriented east–west. The larger slab was said to have covered a rectangular stone-lined grave containing the skeleton of an adult male. At either end of the slab (now in three pieces) is a cupmark immediately enclosed by a circle, each at the centre of a Greek cross. The smaller slab looked as if it had fallen from a standing position and was not found to be covering anything. It bears a cupmark enclosed by two concentric circles and there are traces of a herringbone design. Two free-standing crosses were also found. The function of the enclosure is unknown. Perhaps it was specifically reserved for ecclesiastics within a larger cemetery. Outside the west and east sides of the enclosure 'hundreds' of skeletons were found interred in rectangular pits. No church was recorded at this site, unless the small enclosure described above was the remains of such, but it seems likely that this is the remains of a church site from which the townland name Kilbride derives.

Kilcroney

Kilcroney means the 'church of St Cróne', a female saint who is supposed to have belonged to the family of Niall of the Nine Hostages and to have been related to St Columba. On the site are the remains of a simple rectangular church (10.75m east–west by 6m north–south internally). The partially reconstructed walls survive to a height of 1.5–4.5m. The east gable has the remains of antae, though these were removed during the extension of the church westwards. At the east end of the south wall is a fine example of a small round-headed window. The doorway (1.88m high and 76cm wide) in the south wall is flat-lintelled and has an internal architrave. Perhaps this door was located in the west gable of the original church, and subsequently, when the church was extended westwards, was transferred to the south wall.

Eugene O'Curry, who visited the site in 1837, was fascinated more by an ancient fallen yew tree, of which a branch had continued to grow unhindered, reaching the same diameter (6ft) as the trunk of the original tree. He claimed: 'This tree I look upon as an interesting piece of antiquity'.

Kilgobbin

The name of this church, which stands high on a knoll near the village of Stepaside, refers to St Gobban, though several saints with this name are mentioned in historical texts. Perhaps it is called after the St Gobban who was a nephew of St David of Wales, which may explain why the church was also referred to as *tech na Bretnach*, the 'house of the Welshmen', suggesting that this was a Welsh foundation. The present church on the site is of historic rather than archaeological interest and was built at the turn of the eighteenth century by Archbishop King, but it appears to stand on the site of a pre-Norman church described as being in ruins in 1615. Austin Cooper visited the church in 1781 and wrote: 'I found three holes dug in it. The people there say, it was done at night by some Dublin people—they imagine, they found something, & go so far as to say, that they saw the impression of a Crock in one of the Holes.'

During a clean-up operation of the graveyard some years ago a number of important finds were made, including a complete Rathdown slab and a fragment of another, as well as a fragment of a cross head and half of an upper rotary quern (50cm in diameter), indicating that milling was taking place on site. The complete Rathdown slab (1.6m long, 41–46cm wide and 10cm thick) bears an incised saltire cross and a central line (similar to examples found at

Pl. 76—West face of Kilgobbin high cross.

Whitechurch and Rathfarnham). The slab is round-headed and is very similar to later medieval grave-markers, perhaps indicating that it was reused at this time or that it is a late example of this type of grave-slab.

Presently situated outside the church, beside the lane, is a granite high cross, 2.45m high; the south arm has broken, and the cross was originally 1.18m across. The shaft is decorated with roll-mouldings. On the east face is a carved figure of Christ in a long ankle-length robe with outstretched arms. Rope-moulding descends from beneath the feet to the base, where it divides and extends in opposing directions. On the west face a rather similar depiction of Christ but with shorter arms may represent the Risen Christ or Christ in Glory. This style is more typical of twelfth-century crosses. The cross is inserted in a circular stone (1.45m in diameter) with a bullaun on the south side.

In 1837 John O'Donovan recorded the former existence near the church of a holy well known as Tobernasool (*Tobar na súil*, 'the well of the eyes'), the waters of which may have cured eye infections. The well had already been drained off in O'Donovan's time.

Killegar

Between Enniskerry and the Scalp lies the church site of Killegar, with an impressive view southwards towards the Great Sugar Loaf. The name means 'the Church of Edgar', a Saxon or Welsh name. However, the Book of Leinster associates this site with St Finbar, related to St Berchán of Shankill. By 1219 the church had been assigned to St Patrick's Cathedral, Dublin.

The remains at this site are poorly preserved. Only the grass-covered foundations of the nave survive (approximate original dimensions 12.5m east–west by 5m north–south internally). Of the chancel only the long walls survive (6.5m east–west and 4.3m north–south internally). These walls consist of roughly coursed, mortared granite blocks, which remain unchanged since Eugene O'Curry's visit in December 1838. Though the walls survive to a height of 2m they do not preserve any architectural details such as windows or doorways to provide a date for the building. However, when Liam Price visited the site in 1931 he noticed a granite round-headed window lintel, now lost. Presumably this belonged to either the nave or chancel of the present building at the site, suggesting a twelfth- or early thirteenth-century date for part of the church remains. Traces survive of a surrounding oval enclosure (100m east–west and 80m north–south), consisting of an earth and stone bank (2.5m thick and 1m high).

There are several important finds from the site, including two rotary quern fragments, an undecorated cross base (54cm square and 30cm high), and the remains of a Tau cross. Each broad face of the Tau cross is decorated at the intersection of the arms with a raised circular boss surrounded by a raised ridge. A bronze-coated iron bell (20cm high), probably dating from between 700 and 900, was found in the graveyard and is presently kept in the National Museum of Ireland. During a visit to this site by the Royal Society of Antiquaries in 1897 a conical capstone of a high cross (now lost), typical of the Ahenny group in Tipperary, was mentioned as lying in the graveyard. There is a tradition that Father O'Dwyer, the first parish priest of the Enniskerry parish established in 1860, used a Vatican map to find a large gold cross which had been buried in the graveyard. Nothing is known of what happened to this cross, which may have been a processional cross.

There are also three impressive examples of Rathdown slabs. The decoration on the largest consists of a Latin cross in high relief with cupmarks

Pl. 77—Remains of a Tau cross at Killegar.

on each arm and one at the intersection. The sides of the slab are decorated with small incised arcs, and two small projections from the upper end of the slab form vestigial cross arms. Another slab has two sets of two concentric circles. The lower set is enclosed by a rectangle, while three short lines radiate upwards from the upper set. The smallest slab has a cupmark with two concentric circles, above which is a plain incised Latin cross with radiating diagonal lines. Also from this site comes an interesting Fassaroe-type cross with a Crucifixion in relief on one side, and a cupmark and concentric circle on the other face. This appears to represent a hybrid between the Fassaroe type of crosses and the Rathdown slabs.

In the files of the National Museum of Ireland are very brief records of a cemetery of at least 40 slab-lined graves found during sand-quarrying north of the church site in 1927–8. Apparently the graves were arranged in rows running north–south, buried in the Christian manner with the heads to the west. The fills of some of the graves produced debris, probably associated with the nearby ecclesiastical site, including sherds of early medieval pottery known as souterrain ware, generally found only in the north-east of Ireland. A spindle-whorl found in the fill of one grave suggests textile manufacture at the site.

In 1891 the Rev. Professor Stokes wrote that Killegar 'is a rare spot for a picnic combined with an archaeological excursion, and there is a stream of the coolest water flowing from the ancient Church well'.

Killiney

Presently situated among the grand houses on Killiney Hill are the ruins of a church known in Irish as *cill-inghene-Léinín*, 'the church of Leinin's daughters'. The daughters were Aiglend, Machain, Luiden, Druiden, Lucell, Rimtech and Brigit. Their brother, Colmán mac Léinín, a professional poet before becoming a monk, was the founder of Cloyne, Co. Cork, and died about 604.

The present church building is multi-period. The original church is a single-phase nave and chancel, probably dating from the mid-twelfth century or slightly later. The small chancel arch (1.43m wide and 2.05m high) separates the nave from the tiny chancel (3.5m east–west by 2.8m north–south). The western doorway has inclined jambs and a flat lintel with a Greek cross (40cm by 45cm across) carved in low relief on the soffit. This compares well with a cross carved on the soffit of a similar doorway at Our Lady's Church at Glendalough, possibly established for nuns, and it may be no coincidence that the Killiney church was dedicated to the seven holy daughters of Léinín.

At a later stage, probably during the fifteenth century, an aisle was added to the north of the original church, also with a west doorway (now collapsed), and a fine pointed-arched doorway was inserted into the north wall. In the east wall there is a round-headed window. Its lintel is carved of a single piece of granite, but it does not appear to sit properly on its jambs, suggesting that it has been reused and carelessly reconstructed. Probably during the sixteenth century a two-light, flat-lintelled window was inserted into the south wall of the existing nave in order to bring more light into the enlarged building.

Recently secured to the north long wall is a small Latin granite cross, 44cm high, 33cm across and 11cm thick. The intersection of the cross is raised slightly and may represent a disfigured carved face. Nearby at ground level is a granite font. The basin is 28cm across at the top and a maximum of 30cm deep. Wakeman at the end of the last century recorded that near the church there was once a carn (a station or altar) which was considered sacred by the local people, and was overshadowed by a 'hoary thorn-tree'. He also mentioned an 'earthen rath by which the venerable cemetery was environed', and which has been replaced by a modern stone wall.

Among those buried at the graveyard was James Goodman of Loughlinstown Castle, who in 1576 declared: 'perfect of mynde do make my last will—my bodie to be buried in the church of Killeninge'. According to a note made by Colonel Charles Pratt on the rear of a sketch he made of the church around 1825, two of George Petrie's children, George and Agnes, were buried under a certain tree.

Kill o' the Grange

The original name of this ecclesiastical site was Clonkeen, which may translate as *cluain coain*, 'the quiet meadow'. The site appears to have been dedicated to St Fintan, perhaps one of the sons of Aiglend (one of the seven daughters of Léinín associated with Killiney). However, in the last century Wakeman recorded that the land in the immediate vicinity was referred to by the older local people as 'Mimoge' or 'Moymoge', i.e. 'the plain of Mogue'. St Mogue, also known as St Moling, was an early saint (d. 624) who was bishop of Ferns, Co. Wexford. The Annals of Ulster record that in the year 881 Crunnmael of

Pl. 78—Killiney church.

Cluain Chaín, a bishop and anchorite, 'fell asleep' (died). The church was granted to the Priory of the Holy Trinity by Donough, son of Donald Grossus, shortly before the Anglo-Norman invasion. In 1542 John Callan was appointed vicar, followed by John Hore in 1561.

The nave of this church dates from the tenth or eleventh century. It was a rectangular building with antae projecting 28cm beyond the gable walls. These can still be clearly seen at the west end, where the original doorway is typically flat-lintelled with inclining jambs. The chancel, despite being a later addition, is almost collapsed, except for the east gable, which contains an early thirteenth-century round-headed window. It appears that opposing round-headed windows were inserted high up at the east end of the nave in order to provide additional light, in the absence of an east window. The two-light belfry may have been added to the west gable at a slightly later stage, and a new pointed-arched door constructed nearby in the south wall. In 1630 the church was described as unroofed by recent storms.

A cross-inscribed stone, now missing, was described by Paddy Healy as circular and bearing a slightly sunken Greek cross, above which was a socket, possibly to secure a small free-standing cross. The antiquarian O'Reilly in 1901 described and photographed a small triangular stone bearing an equal-armed cross, 13cm wide, with splayed terminals, also lost.

Also from the site come two small granite crosses, possibly dating from the tenth or eleventh century (recently removed by the Office of Public Works). One has an upright head boss at the intersection of the arms. This cross appears to have been originally associated with the large, undecorated, cube-shaped granite base now in the nave of the church but which originally stood beside the old lane. The second cross head has a boss enclosed by a ring and is associated with the large base still situated beside the north wall of the church.

South-east of the church site, on the green, is a large earthfast boulder with two deep bullauns (34cm and 36cm in diameter, both 36cm deep). Presently only one is visible, the other being hidden below ground level. Also below ground level are the letters 'D O M' inscribed below the bullauns (perhaps representing *Deo Optimo Maximo*), recorded by Wakeman at the end of the nineteenth century, though Liam Price later thought the markings were natural. A nearby holy well, now filled in, was recorded by Wakeman as an oval stone structure which may originally have been covered by roofing flags. The well, then dry, was referred to locally as the British Well.

Kilmacanogue

There is little to indicate the foundation of St Mochonoc (who had strong associations with Glendalough) in the village of Kilmacanogue, at the foot of the Great Sugar Loaf. The present church ruins are smothered in ivy. The south wall and gables of the nave (7.35m east–west by 5.3m north–south internally) remain standing, and represent the earliest surviving church building on the site. The north wall appears to extend slightly (10cm) beyond the west gable, suggesting the presence of antae that may have been removed when the church was extended eastwards. The west gable, usually the location of the doorway, has a fine round-headed window (late twelfth- or early thirteenth-century). At some later stage the east gable was broken through to allow the insertion of an arch (2m wide and 2.25m high), and a chancel was added eastwards. Only the east gable of the small chancel (5.3m east–west) remains; its defaced window was probably originally Gothic in form. When Eugene O'Curry visited the site in 1838 there was a granite pointed-arched doorway with draw-bar hole at the south-west angle of the nave and a little belfry perched on the middle gable, both probably added in Norman times; they have since collapsed.

Kilmashogue

The location of the church site preserved in the townland name Kilmashogue in south Dublin remains a mystery. A granite cross-slab (70cm long), apparently from this townland and probably associated with the church site, bears a Greek cross in a circle, both defined by a raised outline. The narrow shaft is decorated with a narrow raised line forming two loops and another forming a square. This form of cross-slab may date from before the tenth century. After the Norman invasion the lands here (then also known as Baliardor) were held by the Priory of the Holy Trinity.

Kilmurry North

Located on the south-eastern shoulder of the Great Sugar Loaf, overlooking the Glen of the Downs among a grove of ash trees, are the remains of the church which is probably the site mentioned in the *Crede Mihi* list of about 1280 as *Ecclsia de Glinkapyl*. Kilmurry (*cill Mhuire*), 'St Mary's Church', probably derives its name from the ownership of the land in late medieval times by the Cistercian Abbey of St Mary's in Dublin. All that remains are the boulder foundations of a building (11.8m east–west by 6.9m north–south externally). The entrance is at the west end, with a bullaun stone beside it. The water in this stone was believed to cure warts.

On the other side of the road which skirts the church site at the west are the obscured remains of a rectangular enclosure known as Teetemple (*tigh teampuill*, 'the house of the church'), perhaps the remains of a late medieval grange of the monks of St Mary's Abbey, who owned the nearby church. The church was also known locally as Calary (*ceallúrach*, 'disused graveyard'), which lends its name to the neighbouring townland. South-west of the church Eugene O'Curry recorded a holy well called Bride's Well, at which patterns were held until the end of the eighteenth century. This may indicate that the church in pre-Norman times was dedicated to St Brigid and had links with the famous monastery of Kildare.

Kiltiernan

At Kiltiernan (*cill Tighearnáin*) above the Loughlinstown River are the quiet remains of a church which at first glance looks like an early form of rectangular church (14.63m east–west by 7.32m north–south) dating from the eleventh century, as suggested by the straight-lintelled doorway at the west end. However, it seems possible that the west gable and door may belong to an earlier church, and that the rest was added on at a later stage. The masonry of the west gable features some large stones typical of the construction of the earliest stone churches, whereas the east gable, with its small round-headed window, was constructed with much smaller stones possibly at the end of the twelfth century or the beginning of the thirteenth. Curiously, two of the stones of the west door have a chamfer like that found on the east window, which may have been applied when the church was enlarged. Between 1186 and 1195 Donald MacGillaMoCholmóc granted the church at Kiltiernan to St Mary's Abbey, as well as adjoining lands called Tyssoch, Kamas and Baliofelennan, names now obsolete. It was probably shortly after this time that the church was extended. During the fifteenth or sixteenth century a pointed-arched doorway was inserted into the west end of the south wall, forming part of a later porch.

Pl. 79—Kilmurry bullaun stone.

Presently sitting on the sill of the east window of the church is a granite font, possibly of twelfth-century date. This dome-shaped stone is slightly oval at the base (50cm by 53cm) and has a cone-shaped font, 26cm by 28cm at the top and 30cm deep, tapering to a narrow drain hole at the base. Recently found in the graveyard by the author is a fragment of a Rathdown slab bearing a simple incised cross and which has broken across a large cupmark (13.2cm in diameter and 2cm deep).

Kiltuck

In Shanganagh Demesne are the faint traces of a church site, perhaps named after Toca mAeda mSenaich, brother to Crimthann Cualann, king of Leinster, who died in AD 633. All that remains are the foundations of a church, 10.6m east–west by 5.49m north–south. The small twelfth-century Fassaroe-type cross now at St Ann's Church in Shankill originally came from this site and was located east of the church. It has a wheel-shaped head with small projecting arms, and has a Crucifixion scene in false relief on one face, the other side being plain except for the carving of a head in high relief. The top of the cross was found at the church, but curiously the shaft was found in 1938 by workmen repairing the nearby house known as Shanganagh Castle. When Eugene O'Curry visited the site in 1837 he noticed the arch of a window or door, and at that time the cross now located beside a lane in Rathmichael stood here.

Newcourt

Situated at the edge of a golf-course on the southern slopes of Bray Head, with a fine view over much of Bray and south Dublin, are the remains of the small rectangular church known as *rathín a chluig*, the 'little fort of the bell'. The long walls of this small church (10.8m north-west/south-east by 5.9m north-east/south-west) are largely reconstructed, but the gables are quite intact and each contains a small thirteenth-century round-headed window. The tradition of a bell preserved in the placename suggests that this was a church which served the local parish, but its location on Bray Head appears to be well away from any large-scale settlement in the area. It may be no coincidence that the church formed part of the endowments of the Friary of Augustinian Hermits at Dublin (donated by the Archbolds). In 1838 Eugene O'Curry noted traces of two buildings to the east, and he found the remains of a mote or ditch which he believed originally enclosed these structures and the church.

Pl. 80—
Kiltuck
Cross.

Old Connaught

The church ruins at Old Connaught, near Bray, are typical of late medieval parish churches. The site is not associated with any saint, and is first conclusively mentioned by Archbishop Alen in 1615, when it was in good repair. It is a simple rectangular building (10.6m east–west by 5.8m north–south). There is a fine pointed-arched window in the east gable, and a bellcote at the west end. A door in the south wall, now collapsed, was described by D'Alton in 1838 as round-arched, and one of the lintels can still be found lying within the

ruins of the church. There are two ambries in the south wall, and at the east end over the altar are two opposing splayed windows in the north and south walls.

Pl. 81—The church ruins at Old Connaught.

Oldcourt

Outside Bray at Oldcourt is an impressive carved base of a high cross. Eugene O'Curry was informed in 1838 that the cross base was found around 1780 in a hedge beside the nearby road from Bray to Oldcourt Avenue, just where the two townlands meet, and that around that time the cross was moved to below and east of the tower-house in Oldcourt. The cross is illustrated in drawings by Captain Edward Jones in November 1815, and by Du Noyer in August 1840.

The granite base is 1.13m high and measures 80cm by 72cm at the base, tapering towards the top. On the top is a mortice to take the shaft of the cross, which has never been found. Three faces of the base are divided into two compartments with roll-mouldings. The upper compartments appear not to have been sculpted. However, the lower compartments feature a series of carved scenes depicting stories from the Scriptures.

The east face features the Last Judgement, with a winged St Michael holding weighing scales, and Daniel in the Lions' Den. The south face features a hunting scene—a man with a stick or spear and dog apparently hunting or herding four large animals, including a boar, a deer and a large goose. On the upper left are two crossed animals, possibly two horses in combat, while the upper right depicts two figures, one short and one tall, which may represent Cain and Abel, or possibly David and Goliath. On the west face are two large affronted horned animals, one perhaps winged, and between them is a triquetra knot which may represent the Trinity. On this face are also Adam and Eve standing beneath the tree, and an unidentified mounted horseman blowing a horn.

Many of the scenes (in particular Adam and Eve, and Daniel in the Lion's Den) compare well with scenes on other Irish high crosses, such as those from Kells, Castledermot, Moone and Monasterboice, to name a few.

Rarely do such highly decorated ecclesiastical sculptures occur outside a well-known early monastery, and it is unfortunate that there is no other trace of a monastic site at Oldcourt. A cross-slab was also found north of the Dargle on Castle Street in Bray. The sandstone slab (39cm long) has a simple incised cross with barred terminals, below which is a curious incised abstract design. Presently in the Hunt Museum in Limerick city is an example of an early ecclesiastical hand-bell, datable to AD 700–900, which was found somewhere in Bray. The old texts mention three old churches in the Bray area, one in Bray itself at St Paul's. The other two churches, called *Daur Teach* ('oak church') and *Cill easpuig Sillán* ('church of Bishop Sillán'), have not been located (perhaps they were one and the same?). The cross-slab and bell from Bray and the Oldcourt cross base may have belonged to any of these churches.

Rathfarnham

On the outskirts of the village of Rathfarnham, overlooking the River Dodder, is the site of a church first mentioned in 1225. The present remains are of a relatively recent parish church, but the find of a Rathdown slab in the graveyard suggests that this is the site of an earlier, pre-Norman church. The tapering granite slab, found in the north-east corner of the graveyard, is 1.72m long and is broken across one end. It is decorated with six lines which radiate from the centre of the slab, forming a saltire cross. Several semicircular arcs decorate the edges of the slab, and at the broad end are two cupmarks. The slab compares well with examples found at Kilgobbin and Whitechurch.

Rathmichael

The peaceful ruins of this once-important ecclesiastical site appear to be dedicated to St Michael, patron saint of seafarers, favoured by the Christian Hiberno-Norse. The Barnewalls of Shankill Castle and the Walshes of Shanganagh Castle are supposed to have been buried here in the later medieval period.

All that remains of the church are the east gable of a thirteenth-century chancel, with a pointed-arched window, and the south wall of the nave (16.5m long). The chancel arch collapsed in 1852 but can be seen in a sketch made by Colonel Charles Pratt in 1840, and in another sketch made by George Petrie some time before 1819 portions of the north walls of the nave and chancel can be seen still standing. The window in the south wall is a reminder of the use of this church at the beginning of the early modern period, when the nave was extended westwards and a buttress added to the outside of the wall for support. However, the east end of this long wall of the nave (before it was extended westwards) may date back to the twelfth century, and the two twelfth-century round-headed window lintels found in the graveyard may have belonged to this earlier nave.

Alternatively, these round-headed window lintels may belong to the round tower which once stood, typically, west of the church. Only the base remains of this structure, standing only 2m high, but it was probably originally a tall, majestic belfry reaching for the heavens. The reason why this tower fell or was demolished is unknown, but it may subsequently have provided an important source of stone for the later alterations made to the church. This is the only example known of a round tower in the Rathdown area. In the nineteenth century it was popularly known as the Skull House because human bones found during grave-digging were placed within its interior rather than being re-interred. The tower has changed little since it was visited by Austin Cooper in 1778.

According to tradition there was an underground passage leading from under the tower to the sea, and a piper who descended into the passage playing sweet music on his pipes never returned to the surface. This may be the same passage described by Eugene O'Curry in 1837, which consisted of an 'underground passage to the north-west of the site, never explored, stone sides and covered with large flag stones'. Traces of the passage still survive *c.* 30m north-west of the church. This may have been a feature known as a souterrain, a place of refuge, also used as a cool-house for the storage of food.

The site is perhaps best known for its large collection of Rathdown slabs,

Pl. 82—
Rathmichael
church, east
window.

several of which were drawn by George Petrie and George Victor Du Noyer in the nineteenth century. Today there are nine examples secured to the south face of the south wall. Another example was described at the beginning of the century but has not since been located. Two of the slabs presently at the site have two sets of cupmarks enclosed by three incised concentric circles, and the upper set of concentric circles on each slab features short lines radiating upwards. One particularly long, slim stone has a central raised band with four cupmarks, and radiating from the raised band are a series of short incised lines. Two fragments of different slabs are dominated by a herringbone pattern.

Within the church is a fragment of a holy water stoup, as well as a large holed granite slab of unknown function which presently lies against the east gable interior. A broken cross-slab recorded from the site, bearing a Greek cross in a circle carved in relief, is unfortunately now missing. Beside the lane leading to the graveyard, opposite the entrance to a private house, is a bullaun within an earthfast boulder.

The inner enclosing element of the site can be seen to the east of the church as a low, grass-covered embankment. The site is still surrounded by the remains of an outer enclosure (estimated diameter 130m), consisting of a stone wall (1.3m high), with an entrance at the east defined by two large stones.

Beside an old lane in Rathmichael is a Fassaroe-type cross (82cm high), set in an uncarved granite boulder base. The base appears to be in its original location, but the cross itself was found at the church remains at Kiltuck. The cross, re-erected here around 1910, is unusual in that there is a Crucifixion scene on both faces, one in high relief and the other in false relief. It has been suggested that it may mark a route between the church at Rathmichael (400m north-west of the cross) and the ruins of a church at Kiltuck. Alternatively, the cross may mark the site of a church dedicated to St Berchán and known as Shankill, which is the name of the neighbouring townland. Another possibility is that a church, now lost, known as *Cill Comghaill* was located here.

Tonygarrow

At Tonygarrow near Glencree are the remains of a burial-ground once known as *Ros an tSéipéil*, 'wood of the church', possibly referring to the situation of the church near the royal forest that once existed at Glencree. These may be the remains of a church called in the old texts *Cell Crithaich*, 'church of the morass'. In 1838 Eugene O'Curry described a cairn '6 yards long, and 2 yards broad', locally known as a Giant's Grave, which he thought looked like the 'site of some small building'. Liam Price visited the site in 1937, when the cairn was reduced to a low, grass-covered mound, known locally as 'the Rossán' and the 'Bishop's Grave'. O'Curry also found a bullaun stone at the base of an ancient holly tree, of which he wrote: 'Tradition has it that after the destruction of the Chapel, a bell remained suspended from this holly tree, which rung itself on a certain time on the Sabbath, and that some sacrilegious person having lept off one of the branches of the tree, the sacred bell flew off to the top of Glencullen mountain, and buried itself in its bog, and was never since heard of'. The bullaun (40cm across by 18cm deep) is still used to cure warts, and is located in the south-west of an enclosure (40m north–south by 35m east–west) defined by an earth and stone bank and a stream at the north.

Tully (Laughanstown)

Tully, in Laughanstown near Cabinteely, is referred to in the annals as *tulach na n-Epscop*, 'the hill of the bishops'. The Book of Lismore tells of a visit paid to St Brigid of Kildare by eight bishops of Uí Briúin Cualann from 'Telach-na-nEpscop'. Tully may therefore have been an important diocesan centre from an early stage in the history of the Irish church. However, it is highly unlikely that this visit to St Brigid ever occurred, and it seems more likely that Tully came under the wing of Kildare during the eighth century, long after the death of Brigid. Shortly before the Anglo-Norman invasion the church at Tully and the surrounding lands were granted to Christ Church in Dublin by Sitric Mac Torcaill.

Only the foundations of the early nave survive, with a fine arch dividing it from the chancel which was added to the east end during the late twelfth or early thirteenth century. The chancel (5.8m north–south) is unusual in that it is wider than the nave (4.6m north–south), and directly above the chancel arch are the remains of a window, suggesting that the earlier church may have had an upper chamber, perhaps the residential area of the bishop or abbot. The altar was lit by two round-headed east windows and opposing round-headed windows in the north and south walls.

In a field to the north-west is a twelfth-century granite high cross (2.2m high) depicting a figure of a bearded bishop (St Laurence O'Toole?) wearing a full-length garment and holding a crosier. On the west face there are strong raised mouldings outlining the cross, with a featureless head at the intersection of the arms.

However, there are some important traces of the earlier foundation at the site. The nave of the present church probably dates from the end of the eleventh century. The church appears to have been enclosed by a roughly circular enclosure, the line of which is preserved by the modern drystone wall at the east and south-east. Aerial photographs have revealed cropmarks indicating the subsurface presence of two concentric, circular enclosure ditches, with an entrance at the south-east. The twelfth-century high cross described above appears to be located on the western periphery of the outer enclosure. Overlooking the adjoining lane is a granite ringed high cross (2.32m high), possibly dating from the early tenth century. The top has been shaped into a gabled roof with shingles and finials at the ends. The base has an incised Latin cross with barred terminals. Found between the church and the graveyard gate was a small rectangular stone bearing faint traces of a Greek outline cross in a circle, carved in low relief.

Four Rathdown slabs from the site have been removed for safekeeping by the Office of Public Works. One is perhaps the finest example from the series. It bears a central band on which are three sets of concentric circles. The rest of the slab is filled in with a herringbone design. Two small projections from the upper end of the slab form vestigial cross arms. Another slab features a Latin ringed cross in relief with cupmarks on each arm as well as one at the intersection, and a domed boss under each arm. Each side of the cross shaft is filled in with a herringbone design. More recently another example was found in the graveyard, deeply buried in an upright position. At one end there is a cupmark enclosed by three concentric circles. Several lines radiate from the circles, and at one end diagonal and transverse lines form a rough herringbone design. In 1901 the antiquarian O'Reilly described a 'small oval-shaped fragment of stone 5" long by 5.7" thick, bearing a cup-mark 3 $\frac{3}{4}$" wide and 1" deep, and an equal-armed incised cross 3" wide'. Unfortunately, this example has not since been located.

Whitechurch

The patron saint of this site is not known, but its original name was *cill fhuinseann*, and Elizabeth O'Brien has suggested that this may refer to a church of ash wood here. The church was also known as Balgeeth, and its present name derives from the white robes worn by the monks of St Mary's Abbey, to whom the church was granted around 1189. In Strongbow's charter of 1174 it was called Lessnahuinsenn, preserving the Irish word *lios*, 'fort', perhaps referring to an enclosure around the church. The church and neighbouring lands were granted by Strongbow to Thomas Flandrensis (the Fleming), but were later given by the Crown to Robert de Saint Michael, whose son David de St Michael together with Milo de Stanton donated many of the lands, including Harold's Grange, to St Mary's Abbey.

D'Alton, writing in 1838, found only 'the wall dividing the aisle and chancel standing', and much of the present building appears to represent a more recent reconstruction of a late sixteenth-century church. However, several finds testify to the antiquity of the site. A Rathdown slab was found near the present entrance, buried deeply in an upright position. It features a saltire cross with a cupmark at the intersection and a form of herringbone design. Also found in the graveyard was a tapering granite cross-slab, 1.5m long, bearing some similarities to the Rathdown series of grave-slabs. It bears a Greek cross in a circle, and the four quadrants are slightly recessed. There is a small cupmark at the intersection. This cross forms part of a Latin cross in low relief. Below the arms of this cross are two raised bosses, similar to slabs from Fairy Hill and Tully. Unfortunately, a font mentioned by D'Alton in 1838 has now disappeared.

Beside the road leading south from Whitechurch to Kilmashogue is an earthfast boulder known as the Wart Stone. The hole within the stone, which is frequently filled with rainwater, is in fact a mortice (41cm by 28cm) to hold a free-standing cross, now lost. Adjacent to the mortice is an inscription consisting of the letters 'I L' and an incised cross with slightly splayed terminals. Could this cross have marked the site of a nearby monastic mill, or the boundary between Kilmashogue and Whitechurch?

Castles

Bullock Castle

Strategically overlooking Dalkey Sound is the imposing edifice of Bullock Castle. This is a fine example of a tower-house, probably built during the fifteenth century. Unfortunately, there is no historical reference to tell us who built this castle, though it is generally believed to have been built to protect the fishing rights of the monks of St Mary's Abbey, who owned the land here as part of their manor at Monkstown. Another possibility is that the castle was built, or at least lived in, by the Walsh family, who had gradually become powerful in the area during the fifteenth century. The Walshes had taken over the office of water-bailiff, keeping for themselves all profits levied from those using the port at Colliemore Harbour, money that was due to the archbishop. What better way to take control of this lucrative position than to build a castle overlooking those ships using Dalkey Sound? In the late sixteenth century the castle was owned by two brothers, Christopher and Richard Fagan, who lived at Feltrim, and both became mayor of Dublin. In the eighteenth century a three-storey house was added on to the south-east side of the castle. The building was demolished during the 1980s but is preserved in a sketch made by Colonel Charles Pratt in 1813, at which time there were also several thatched cottages around the base of the castle at the east and north-east. The castle is shown in its full glory in a pen and wash drawing by Francis Place in 1698.

Pl. 83—Bullock Castle.

The tower-house is now refurbished and fitted with modern windows. The ground floor is vaulted, and projecting beyond the north-east wall is a tower containing the narrow spiral staircase. In the last century, the pleasant gate arch at the north-west gave access to the courtyard of the castle, which was enclosed by a bawn wall. There was also a fine square watch-tower. No trace now remains of either this bawn wall or the watch-tower, but they are shown on a 1766 painting by Gabriel Beranger. The bawn wall extended from the tower-house for about 100m towards Dalkey, probably along the line of the modern road. It terminated at the small tower, now gone, and then turned downhill towards the sea. Perhaps the bawn was constructed in the sixteenth century, when the authorities were worried about a Spanish landing here. In the Civil Survey of 1654 the castle was listed as slated. There was a port here then, and the bawn was described as 'a good haven'. Altogether the buildings were valued by the Survey at £100, a healthy sum at that time. The castle is perhaps best known for the carving of a human head, projecting beyond the south-west angle of the tower and looking in the direction of Dalkey village.

Dalkey

Tradition holds that there were seven castles in Dalkey. Today only two survive, Goat's Castle and Archbold's Castle. They were probably constructed at the end of the fifteenth century, when provisions were made to defend the town. Rather than being true castles they probably served as the fortified residences of merchants. The name of Goat's Castle derives from the crest of the Cheevers family, which was a demi-goat, though there is no historical evidence that they ever owned the castle. It was largely remodelled in the nineteenth century as a residence and in the twentieth century as the town hall. Today it serves as a heritage centre, but has changed little since it was painted by Gabriel Beranger in 1766. Built of the colourful local granite, it consists of three floors, and the original vault still extends over the ground floor. Below the vault was a storage area with a wooden floor, forming the ceiling over the ground floor. The original doorway to the castle was at the west end of the north wall, opposite the street front. From this door a stone stair within the thickness of the west wall provides access to the upper chamber. From the upper chamber stones and other deadly objects could be dropped through a 'murder-hole' onto intruders at the bottom of the stairs. At the east end of the upper room is a chamber within the thickness of the north wall which served as a garderobe. A short flight of stone steps provides access to the wall-walk around the battlements surrounding the roof. Here are two turrets, and also two machicolations projecting slightly beyond the battlements, one directly above the door. These enabled the defenders to hide from the archers of the assailants and to protect the door below.

Archbold's Castle is a fifteenth-century towerhouse, though it appears that the Archbolds never owned it. This may be the castle granted in 1585 to John Dongan, together with half an orchard and two acres of land. Dongan was a merchant and government official, who served three terms as lord mayor and one as city sheriff. The ground floor (3.8 wide, north–south) of the castle is vaulted, and a line of joist holes indicate that a ceiling once separated the ground floor from the vault; this area was probably used for storage. Access was gained to this room and the floor above by a stone stair within the thickness of the north wall. The lintel of the doorway to the storage room is in fact a cross-inscribed grave-slab from the graveyard across the street. On the top floor there is a fine fireplace in the west wall. The roof no longer survives, but the narrow wall-walk is still accessible by the staircase to a turret in the roof. Projecting from the battlements is a machicolation protecting the door to the castle. The earliest known painting of the castle, by Gabriel Beranger in 1766, shows the remains of a building added onto the west side of the castle at some time. High up on the west wall, just below the chimney, a piece of plaster preserves traces of the gable pitch of this building. A woodcut of Beranger's original accompanied Peter Wilson's 'A topographical description of Dalkey and the environs' in *Exshaws Magazine* (1770). This is one of only a few of Beranger's paintings published in his lifetime.

Wilson was the first to mention the tradition of seven castles in Dalkey, and he described them as follows: 'One of the castles has been repaired, and, by means of some additional buildings, converted into a commodious habitation. A second has been roofed and affords room for a good billiard table. A third and fourth are inhabited by publicans; indeed the most antique and complete of the whole is occupied by a stable. A sixth, or rather the small remains of it, may be found in the walls of an old cabin. And the seventh has been totally demolished a few years ago, merely for the sake of the stones.'

Today little is known of where the other five castles once stood. Perhaps fragments were incorporated into the modern buildings in the village and remain to be discovered by future research. Historically we can say that Henry Walsh (d. 1570) of Killincarrig had two castles in Dalkey and 75.5 acres of land. During the fifteenth and sixteenth centuries the Walsh family were a significant influence in the town and controlled the office of water-bailiff, keeping for themselves all profits levied from those using the port at Colliemore Harbour. Perhaps they used some of these funds to construct several of the castles in Dalkey. One of the Walsh castles was located at the east end of the town near the junction between Main Street and St Patrick's Road. One castle, known as the Black Castle, was described by Peter Wilson as affording 'room for a good billiard table'. This may be the castle depicted in a drawing by Francis Grose *c.* 1790 showing the streetscape of Dalkey at that time. Both Archbold's and Cheevers' castles are shown, as well as a castle with crenellated battlements and string-coursing a short distance west of the church. In 1820 only three castles were still standing, which Cromwell described as: 'one forming part of a private house, another being occupied as a house and store, and the third as a forge'. According to Samuel Lewis in 1837 one castle was still used as a residence, one as a store and another as a carpenter's shop. The latter may have been Wolverston's Castle, which originally stood within the angle formed by Ulverton Road and Castle Street, and may have been a gatehouse in the town wall. It took its name from the Wolverston family of Stillorgan, who held property in Dalkey until 1681.

While there is no conclusive evidence that there were ever seven castles in

Dalkey, it is interesting to note that the *Map of the Bay and Harbour of Dublin,* surveyed in 1686 by Captain Greenail Colins, shows Dalkey ringed by a wall fortified with seven towers or bastions. Later maps by Gibson (1756) and Rocque (1760) also show seven castles at Dalkey. Perhaps these maps do record the former existence of seven castles here. However, Colins may have used a certain amount of artistic licence in depicting Dalkey and the later cartographers may simply have copied his earlier map, giving rise to the tradition recorded by Wilson.

Dundrum Castle

The present castle on the outskirts of Dundrum village, overlooking the River Slang, appears to have been built by Richard Fitzwilliam around 1590 on the site of an earlier castle, dating from the turn of the thirteenth century, on land previously granted to the Norman knight John de Clahull, marshal of the lordship of Leinster. The location appears to have been carefully chosen in order to oust a previous landowner who had a fortification in the area, commemorated in the placename Dundrum, *Dun Droma* ('the fort of the ridge').

There were few obvious traces of the earlier castle before excavation by Elizabeth O'Brien. Several seasons of digging have found and recorded features of the original thirteenth-century castle, including the moat that once enclosed the site. This was generally 7m wide and 4.5m deep but narrowed at the gatehouse, where it was crossed by a drawbridge. The ditch does not appear to have contained water, and was gradually backfilled during the thirteenth and fourteenth centuries with rubbish from the castle, including large quantities of green-glazed pottery called Leinster ware and sherds of imported Saintonge pottery, probably containing French wine. Also found during the excavations were large amounts of butchered bone, as well as oyster and cockle shells and the headless skeleton of a pony. This backfilling suggests that the ditch no longer served a defensive purpose in the early fourteenth century, and that Dundrum was a peaceful area shortly before the Gaelic Revival.

Across the moat at the base of an entrance gatehouse was found a well-built pier containing three parallel vertical slots. This would have supported a drawbridge known as a turning bridge, consisting of a wooden platform which extended across the moat. The bridge was raised and lowered using counterweights, which would fit into the slots underneath the gatehouse when the drawbridge was raised. A blocked-up arch of this gatehouse was incorporated into the wall of the later castle.

In the fourteenth century the land was conveyed to the Fitzwilliams by Sir Robert le Bagod of Baggotrath. The present building on the site is a cross between a tower-house and a fortified house, and was probably built by Richard Fitzwilliam around 1590, replacing the earlier castle. According to his will in 1596, Fitzwilliam desired that all his tenants dwelling at Dundrum who assisted him in the construction of the castle should be forgiven rent arrears after his death. There was a watermill here in 1616. About that time Richard Fitzwilliam's son, William, who had married Primate Henry Ussher's widow, lived at the castle. After the 1641 Rebellion the castle came into the possession of Lt. Col. Isaac Dobson, an officer in the Parliamentarian Army. Soon after, he became commissioner for revenue and transplantation for the Civil Survey of 1654–6. Dobson probably improved the castle, and after the Restoration the Fitzwilliams allowed the Dobsons to remain there. According to the Civil Survey, in 1654 the castle was slated and possessed a barn, a garden plot and a small orchard. Altogether, these were valued at £100. Isaac Dobson was succeeded by his only surviving son, Alderman Eliphal Dobson, whose creaking wooden leg, according to tradition, announced his approach wherever he went. He was a wealthy publisher, and the first Bible printed in Ireland bears his name in the imprint.

The present building continued to be lived in throughout the early eighteenth century. A painting by Gabriel Beranger in 1765 shows the castle refurbished with the insertion of many Georgian windows, a slated roof with an impressive chimney block, and the application of pebble-dashing to the exterior. However, the string-coursing and the battlements above appear to be original, and at ground level there are still some fine examples of sixteenth-century musket-loops. At that time the building was L-shaped, consisting of a rectangular tower with a slightly smaller square tower at the north-west, extending over the moat that enclosed the original thirteenth-century castle. In this tower can still be seen the large joist holes for the support timbers of the wooden floors. The kitchen area was located in the main tower, where at ground level there is a large, impressive fireplace (refurbished in the eighteenth century) with an oven hole at the right-hand side. There are further fireplaces, also refurbished, at first- and second-floor level.

At some stage, possibly during the seventeenth century, an extension was added to the north-east wall of the main sixteenth-century tower and partially built on the line of the thirteenth-century castle and its gatehouse. This later building has almost totally disappeared, and one of Beranger's paintings shows that this part of the castle had largely collapsed by 1765. The painting also shows that there were battlements at roof level so that it blended in with the castle.

Fassaroe

Beside a private residence at Fassaroe, overlooking the Dargle valley, are the ruins of a tower-house built by William Brabazon, the treasurer of Ireland, around 1534. A few years later the castle was granted to Peter Talbot. Only the south and west walls survive. In the south wall are the remains of a barrel vault which originally extended over the first floor. The vault and the soffits of the embrasures retain traces of wicker centring. There is no trace of the doorway or stairwell. The bases of the walls were slightly battered. In 1534 there was a watermill and fishery here. The castle was owned by Lord Bernard Talbot at the time of the 1641 Rebellion, when according to folklore it was attacked by Cromwell and his forces.

Kilgobbin Castle

In private grounds at Kilgobbin are the partial remains of a fifteenth-century tower-house, probably constructed by a member of the Walsh family. It was occupied by Morris Walsh in 1482. The north and east walls have largely collapsed. The tall doorway is located at the north end of the west wall, and immediately inside is a square draw-bar hole. South of this door is an arched recess with a narrow slit arrow-loop. The ground floor is spanned by the remains of a high vault, directly below which is a clear line of square joist holes for the supports of a timber floor. In the tower at the south-east there was originally a stone spiral staircase. In 1654 the castle was roofed with thatch. There are few features present on the top floor. A painting by Beranger shows the east side of the castle complete in 1766. In 1780 Austin Cooper was able to climb the stairs up to the battlements. At the south-east corner he found a room in one of the turrets with a 'little Closet with a Nich in it from which there is a hole down to the Ground. I imagine it to have been a Necessary [toilet].' An engraved drawing by George Petrie some time before 1819 shows the castle as well preserved at the beginning of the nineteenth century.

Killincarrig Castle

Killincarrig, between Greystones and Delgany, may originally have belonged to the Sutton family of Kildare (Gilbert de Sutton was sheriff of Kildare in 1297), and the land was probably leased to them in the early fourteenth century by another Kildare family, the de Kenleys, who lived at Kindlestown. The ivy-smothered ruins at Killincarrig represent a Jacobean house built by Henry Walsh of Carrickmines around the turn of the seventeenth century. This is a good example of a fortified house, but many of the architectural details are difficult to make out owing to the overwhelming growth of ivy. The L-shaped, gabled building (14.3m long and 7.6m wide) has two storeys and an attic. Attached to the north-east side is a kitchen block (6.9m by 4.9m internally). The large windows indicate that defence was not a primary concern of the builders, though the stair turret projecting beyond the west wall harks back to the design of earlier tower-houses, and there are several musket-loops at ground level. The door is located in the east wall, and there is a shallow armorial recess overhead. There are two tall chimney stacks, one above the west wall and the other above the north gable. At this time a tax was placed on fireplaces, and the number of chimneys was a reflection of the owner's social status. During the Rebellion of 1641 a woman named Kathleen Farrell was arrested as a spy in the nearby village and sent to Dublin, where she was sentenced to be hanged. In 1655 the Down Survey claimed that 'the most remarkable Building in this halfe Barony is the House of Killingcargie, being garrisoned dureing the time of the late wars'.

Kindlestown

At Kindlestown, near Delgany, are the ruins of a castle which takes its name from Albert de Kenley, sheriff of Kildare, who reputedly built it in 1301. De Kenley may have acquired the land through his marriage to the widow of Ralph FitzJohn, a descendant of Domnall MacGillaMoCholmóc. The Archbolds appear to have occupied the castle by 1315. In 1377 it was seized by the O'Byrnes, but was subsequently recovered by Archbishop Wikeford, then chancellor.

It is a type of castle, rare in Ireland, known as a hall-house. Only the north long wall and the south-east corner of the building survive, and unfortunately the remainder of the castle has been reduced to rubble. It was originally rectangular (17m east–west by 6.3m north–south internally) and was constructed in two phases, as can be seen clearly from outside the castle on the north. A clear change in the masonry (about 5m above ground level) coincides with the upper level of the barrel vault, traces of which can be seen clearly on the interior and which may have served to roof the building for a period. Shortly afterwards, construction of the building continued with the completion of the upper storey. This phase did not incorporate the granite quoins which feature at ground level. Furthermore, the putlog holes which supported the scaffolding used to construct the earlier phase of the castle do not feature above the change in masonry, indicating that a different construction method was used. The reason for the two phases of construction is not clear. Perhaps the original owner, de Kenley, began construction after 1301, but the project was not completed until the Archbolds took possession around 1315.

The living quarters were on the top floor, which was reached by a stair well within a tower, now collapsed, at the north-east angle of the castle. At the west end of the north wall there is a tower with garderobe chutes serving the upper floor and the parapet, and there is a cross-loop at upper floor level in the north-west tower. Within the interior of the castle is a clear line of joist holes that would have supported a timber floor directly beneath the barrel vault; this area lacked windows and was perhaps used for storage. The upper level has square-headed rectangular slit windows with deep embrasures, one preserving a window-seat. At the top of the north wall can be seen a string-coursing and the wall-walk with drain holes around the roof. The roof was at one time covered with purple slates, the fragments of which can still be seen scattered among the rubble. Also among the rubble of the castle the writer found a stone mortar and a fragment of a rotary quern which had been used as building material. Both artefacts are typical of the early medieval period, suggesting that the castle may have been built on or in the vicinity of an earlier settlement site. The castle was originally surrounded by a water-filled moat 4m wide, which was noted by Liam Price in 1930 but is now difficult to detect.

Lehaunstown

The core of the present private dwelling at Lehaunstown House consists of extremely thick walls forming a small rectangular building (measuring 9.5m by 6.5m). These walls are the remains of a castle leased by the Archbolds, who were replaced as tenants by John Graham in 1568. During the 1641 Rebellion the vicar of Rathmichael, the Rev. Simon Swayne, took refuge at Lehaunstown Castle, which was then attacked and set on fire by Robert Barnewall of Shankill and James Goodman of Loughlinstown. Apparently Swayne escaped after being terribly burnt and losing the sight of one eye.

Monkstown Castle

Perhaps one of the most interesting castles in Rathdown is to be found at Monkstown. There is little historical evidence to indicate the original builder of this castle, though it is often considered that the monks of St Mary's Abbey, who owned the land, built the castle also. The earliest recorded owner is John Travers, master of the ordnance and a groom of the chamber to the king, at the time of the dissolution of the monasteries in the 1540s. Travers, from Cornwall, was also granted land at Blackrock. Sir Henry Sidney, on his arrival as lord deputy in 1565, stayed at Monkstown on his way to Dublin from Dalkey. The castle frequently changed ownership, and in 1610 passed into the hands of the Cheevers family. After the 1641 Rebellion, Walter Cheevers was deported to Connacht and the castle was granted to General Edmund Ludlow, Cromwell's master of the horse in Ireland and one of the signatories of the death warrant of Charles I. Ludlow kept 20 horses ready for service in his stables within the castle courtyard. According to the Civil Survey of 1654 there was 'one old castle newly repaired [by Ludlow] with a Barne, Two garden plotts & an Orchard; one Mill', all valued at £300.

There is no trace of the large timber doorway (over 3m high) that one would have passed through into the gatehouse. This building, with its pronounced buttress projecting northwards and a high, pitched vault, has a beautiful example of a mid-fifteenth-century ogee-headed window on the south side, but elsewhere has been marred by the insertion of later red brick windows. The gatehouse once extended to the east, but this section has long since collapsed. Adjacent to the gate are the foundations of a square tower, and the remains of a spiral staircase providing access to it can still be seen. Once through the gatehouse the bawn wall focuses one's attention on the tower-house directly in front. This crenellated wall was almost certainly reconstructed in more recent times, but reflects the line of the original bawn wall.

The castle building itself is a tower-house, probably built in the middle of the fifteenth century, although many of its original features have been replaced during later alterations. It consists of three storeys above ground level. Projecting from the south wall is a tower to accommodate a stone spiral staircase, which still retains two of the original slit arrow-loops. Another arrow-loop can be seen at ground level in the north wall, to defend against anyone attacking the bawn wall. Higher up on the north wall several of the original windows, subsequently blocked up, can still be seen. At the top of the east wall are two chimneys. At the south end of the east wall can be seen the imprint of the demolished bawn wall, which extended eastwards.

Two paintings by Gabriel Beranger in 1766 show that the present tower was one of two at either end of a courtyard, opposite the gate-tower. There is no longer any trace of this second tower. Extending between the two towers was a late seventeenth-century multi-chimneyed mansion, built along the bawn wall and now demolished. This is confirmed by Austin Cooper, who visited the castle in 1780: 'This is a very large Building consisting of two Square Castles with turrets, & one high tower, between which & farther back is built a house, all in Gothic Taste & before it, is a handsome Lawn encompassed with a Shrubbery and Serpentine Walk'. The only evidence of this mansion today can be seen on the east side of the surviving tower-house, where traces of a gable are preserved in the external plasterwork, and at the north-east angle of the tower-house, where a dressed limestone jamb of a door to the mansion can be found. A blocked-up red brick doorway in the tower-house provided access into the mansion at second-floor level. It seems likely that the mansion was built after the Restoration of Charles II in 1660, when the castle was returned to Walter Cheevers. Perhaps it was built shortly after that date, by Archbishop Boyle or his eldest son, Viscount Blessington.

The gardens that once distinguished the grounds of the castle are said to have been commissioned in the middle of the seventeenth century by General Edmund Ludlow, but they are more likely to have been started later. In 1780 the gardens, as well as a shrubbery and serpentine walk, contained ice-houses, ferneries and greenhouses. A small stream once flowed to the east of the castle and originally there may have been a mill here. The stream was described in the Civil Survey of 1654 as 'a small Creek for a haven', and was later dammed to form an artificial fishpond (filled in during the 1960s) as part of the ornamental gardens.

Around the middle of the eighteenth century an extension was added to the west side of the tower-house. This part of the building, which extends beyond the area defended by the bawn wall and which features large windows (now blocked up), may have been built when the castle was owned by Dr Robert Roberts (d. 1758) or by his successor, Mr Robert Erlington. In 1780, when the castle was advertised for sale, it was described as a house in Gothic style, three storeys high, and 'comprised numerous apartments, including a saloon, library, gallery and chapel—the second finest house in south Dublin'. More recently, the castle is supposed to be haunted by a certain Widow Gamble.

There was at least one other castle near Monkstown, the only surviving evidence for which is a painting made in 1771 by Beranger. It was apparently known as Monkstown Castle, and Beranger described it as 'smaller than the first. A private fortified dwelling, inconsiderable if compared to the other.' Beranger shows a long rectangular building, possibly a hall-house castle. It appears to have been located closer to Dun Laoghaire, and in Beranger's time much of this area was also known as Monkstown. On John Rocque's 1760 *Maps of the County* this area was called MonksTown Common, and a large house called Carrilkgouloge is marked. This appears to be a corruption of a building called Corrig Castle on Taylor's 1816 map of *The Environs of Dublin*, and on Duncan's 1821 *Map of the County of Dublin* the castle is shown, though not named, and the surrounding land was called Carricklands. This castle was located near Corrig Park, off Corrig Road near Dun Laoghaire. Unfortunately a building known as Corrig Castle was demolished here some years ago and may have incorporated fragments of the castle, which perhaps defended the route to Dublin from Dalkey and Bullock through Monkstown.

Oldcourt

Standing high on a natural knoll of rock outcrop above a stream is Oldcourt Castle, possibly built by the Archbolds, and later owned by the Walsh family. All that remains of the late fifteenth-century castle is a fine tower, which serviced a two-storey hall (about 16m long and 7.85m wide) attached to its west side. The hall has disappeared, but the pitch of its gable can still be seen in the plaster attached to the west face of the tower. There is no access to the tower at ground level, entry being originally gained from the hall at the first floor through a round-headed doorway. There is a ground floor and three upper storeys, accessed by a spiral stairwell. Barrel vaulting extends across the ground- and first-floor levels. There are fine examples of little ogee-headed windows with glazing bar holes at second-floor level in the east and south walls. The Down Survey map of 1657 shows the tower with a conical roof rising above the battlements and warder's walk. Originally a bawn wall attached to the north-west and south-west corners extended south. The entrance into the bawn was between two circular gate-towers at the south, one of which still stands 2.5m high.

Powerscourt

At the time of the Norman invasion Powerscourt was known as Balitened, and nearby was a church called Stagonil, owned at that time by the archbishop. The original castle was located to the north-west of Powerscourt House, on a natural glacial ridge. The top of this hill (50m east–west by 40m north–south) has been artificially flattened and is probably the site of a (timber?) castle built by Eustace le Poer (Power) before 1302. In 1316 the castle was being repaired by one of the king's officials, and in 1339, when there was general war reported throughout Ireland, Powerscourt was garrisoned and held by a constable appointed by the king. By 1355 the castle was in ruins and the territory was overrun by the O'Tooles, who called this area Fercullen (*Fir Cualann*, 'the men of Cualann'), apparently an ancient name for part of the lands known as Uí Briúin Cualann prior to the Norman invasion. It would seem, therefore, that the O'Tooles revived this name as part of their claims to rightful ownership of the lands in the fifteenth century, though the name Fercullen was probably not used for the Powerscourt region originally. In 1355 Odo O'Toole was allowed by the king to remain at Powerscourt on condition that he preserved the lands from the invasions of the O'Byrnes, but the O'Tooles did not maintain their loyalty for long.

In 1450 the Irish parliament granted permission to Sir Edmond Mulsoe to establish a borough, to be called Mulsoes Court, in north Wicklow on the borderlands. The grant allowed for bailiffs and burgesses, and for customs dues to be used for walling and paving the town. The intended location appears to have been in the Powerscourt area, but the borough was not referred to again. Given that Mulsoe died in 1463, it would appear that he never went ahead with his ambitious project, and the area remained in the possession of the O'Tooles.

A castle, incorporated within the present mansion, was built sometime after 1482 and called Powers Courte by the eighth earl of Kildare, Garret Mór. The earl had been appointed viceroy some years before and emerged as the most powerful figure in Ireland at that time, hailed by some as the uncrowned king of Ireland. His castle at Powerscourt was apparently 'one of the fairest garrysons in this countrie', built at a cost of four or five thousand marks. It later passed into the hands of the ninth earl of Kildare, Gerald, and his brother Richard. The lands of Powerscourt were confiscated following the rebellion of Richard's nephew, Silken Thomas, in 1534. In 1538 an inquisition was held in Dublin to determine the extent of the lands to be confiscated. Among the jurors of the inquisition were Richard Walsh of Kilgobbin, Walter Walsh of Shanganagh, William and Gerald Archbold of Bray, and William Walsh of Killiney.

In 1535 William Brabazon, the treasurer of Ireland, was said to be rebuilding the castle here, but the following year it was reportedly levelled ('prostrated'). Shortly afterwards it was granted to Peter Talbot, who also received Fassaroe and Rathdown. However, Talbot was persuaded to grant Powerscourt to Brian O'Toole (known as Brian *an chogaidh*, 'Brian of the Battles'), and as compensation he received grants of land at Ballycorus, Bullock and Ballyman.

In 1603 Powerscourt Castle was leased to a new English arrival, Sir Richard Wingfield, who had been appointed marshal of Ireland three years earlier and had played an important role in the final capture of the notorious Feagh MacHugh O'Byrne. Later Wingfield was granted the lands for life. In 1731 the earlier castle was incorporated into an estate mansion, which has since been remodelled several times. The house was almost completely destroyed by fire in 1974 and only recently refurbished, the final episode in a long history of destruction and rebuilding at Powerscourt. It is an unfortunate coincidence that the name of the area at the time of the Norman invasion was Balitened, *baile teineadh*, 'town of the fire'.

In 1838 Eugene O'Curry visited Powerscourt and was told stories by a man named George Burton of an Irish rebel named Fiach O'Toole who lived here at the time of Sir Richard Wingfield (there is no record of a rebel by that name at Powerscourt, and perhaps the story is a confusion between Feagh MacHugh O'Byrne and Garrett O'Toole, rebels at the end of the sixteenth century). Burton said: 'Begor, Sir, Fiach O'Toole was a brave Soldier and used to hang every person that could not say Cú, and Maddú (i.e., Hound and Dog) in the Irish language'. Apparently Fiach hung his enemies on a gallows on the mound of the thirteenth-century castle. In the kitchen yard at Powerscourt House, O'Curry was shown a stone-carved human head, allegedly representing Fiach O'Toole, and in his description of the carving he claimed: 'any one who knows Daniel O'Connell well, will immediately think of him on looking at it'.

Puck's Castle

In the townland of Rathmichael is a site which, as the antiquarian D'Alton poetically put it, is 'known by the elfin appellation of Puck's castle'. The origin of the name Puck is unknown, though it may refer to a forgotten ghost (*puca*) that once haunted the residence. Popularly known as a castle, this building is in fact an unfortified house. At first glance it may resemble a tower-house, probably because it was built at a time when such buildings were still in common use, at the end of the sixteenth century. It is a small rectangular building (6.7m east–west by 4.5m north–south internally) of two floors above ground level, and the walls are only 1.3m thick. There are fine garderobes at first- and second-floor level at the east end of the north wall. The chute is within the thickness of the wall and opens at ground level.

The stone stairs are within the west wall, and at their foot at ground level is an arched entrance (2.4m high and 1.4m wide) with a square slot for a large timber beam that would have been drawn across to secure the door. This is the only defensive feature of the castle. That defence was not a priority of the builders is highlighted by the large open windows in the north and south walls, taking advantage of the panoramic view to the north and the sunlight from the south. The north wall has a slight batter at the base, but rather than being a defensive measure this appears to have been designed to support the building because it is built on a slope. The kitchen may have been at ground level, associated with a large fireplace in the east wall that has been broken open.

At some later stage, probably in the early eighteenth century, there were some alterations to the building, including a new brick fireplace at top-floor level in the east wall. Two new doorways were inserted at ground level in the north and south walls. Outside the south wall, at the east end, a chimney flue was inserted into the thickness of the wall for a fireplace belonging to a building (now demolished) added onto this wall. An engraved drawing by George Petrie some time before 1819 shows two thatched houses built onto the south-east angle of the castle.

Rathdown Upper

Overlooking the Irish Sea at Rathdown Upper is the site of a manorial castle which was the seat of the Gaelic lord Domnall MacGillaMoCholmóc. Shortly afterwards the family name was changed to the Norman name FitzDermot. The MacGillaMoCholmóc family were one of the very few native lords to be assimilated into the incoming Norman regime, and had a Dublin street and

Pl. 84—Puck's Castle.

gate named after them up to the fifteenth century. Rathdown Upper was acquired by Nigel le Brun in 1308, though two years later the lands were reported to be waste. This may not have lasted long, and a lively village probably built up around the castle.

The castle is no longer upstanding, and was robbed of its stone during the construction between 1854 and 1856 of the railway (now used as the cliff walk from Bray to Greystones) which skirts the east of the site. It was illustrated on the Down Survey map of 1657 as a single tower, at which time a village of ten cottages stood to the north-north-west. In 1827 G.N. Wright described the ruins at the site: 'the ground plan may be distinctly traced by the heaps of ruinous masonry, now all grass grown, which like lifeless bodies, that occupy the very spot on which they perished, lie regularly and artificially arranged in square and circular and other usual architectural forms. The basement of one large square tower may still be seen, the walls of which are four feet in thickness. In the eastern side was a circular headed window, the architrave of which is yet tolerably perfect.' Soon afterwards Eugene O'Curry visited the site and described it as '54' in length on the S. side and about 8' high—also a small portion of the N. wall'.

The castle stood within the southern half of a large enclosure (43m square) consisting of a large ditch or moat, 4m wide and now only 80cm deep, which survives best at the north and west, and has been almost obliterated along the south by a laneway and at the east by the old railway line. About 7m outside this square ditch was another ditch, 3m wide, which once enclosed the whole site. Both ditches are now almost totally silted up and are difficult to identify on the ground, but can be seen clearly from aerial photography. Both were probably originally filled with water by a stream to the south-west. At the north side access was gained across both ditches by a substantial causeway, 7m wide.

To the south-west of the castle site is St Crispin's Cell, a small rectangular stone church (8.23m east–west by 5.49m north–south). There is a large window opening at the east end, and a round-arched chamfered doorway at the west end. Attached to the west end are the remains of a tiny porch. This building appears to represent an eighteenth-century church, and incorporates the cut stones of a late medieval church. The earliest historical reference to the church is as late as 1530.

According to Weston St John Joyce, writing sometime before 1913, 'The village of Rathdown stood a short distance to the north-west, and in draining one of the fields there during the last century, the remains of a paved street were discovered.' In 1534 there were twenty houses and a watermill here.

Near the castle at Rathdown a hoard was found, consisting of several hundred coins, mostly of Elizabeth I, including 79 shillings and 321 sixpences, as well as a small number of coins from 1553 (Queen Mary) and 1607 (James I). There were also two Spanish *reales* of Ferdinand and Isabella (1469–1504). Also found near the castle site were a late medieval bronze cloak-pin and a small late medieval bronze spearhead (8.5cm long and 1.7cm wide) which still has part of the timber haft embedded within the socket.

Rathfarnham Castle

At Rathfarnham is a fine example of a type of castle known as a fortified house, dating from the end of the sixteenth century. The lands here were granted to Milo le Bret in 1199. They were leased soon after to the Harolds, who remained tenants here until the fifteenth century. In 1320 Milo le Bret, who resided in Cork, leased part of the lands to his legal adviser, John Graunteste, for a yearly rent of 20s. and a robe of proportionate value. His son, John le Bret, sheriff of Cork, was ordered in 1356 to proceed to his manor of Rathfarnham with his followers fully armed, following an attack by the O'Byrnes. The lands changed hands several times, and at the beginning of the fifteenth century reverted to the crown, though the Harolds appear to have remained tenants. Excavations by Judith Carroll to the north of the present castle found the remains of an undercroft (an underground vaulted chamber) of an earlier castle, perhaps built by the Harolds at the beginning of the fifteenth century. In 1423 the manor was divided into two parts, one granted to Thomas Hall in that year, and the second granted to James Cornwalsh, chief baron of the Exchequer, in 1424.

By the end of the sixteenth century the village was described as wasted by the Irish of the mountains. About this time the land was acquired by Archbishop Adam Loftus, who built the present castle here as a stately residence between 1583 and 1585. The archbishop, a native of Yorkshire, was also renowned as lord chancellor and the first provost of Trinity College, Dublin. Loftus established one of the largest estates in Dublin, and by the time of his death he had twenty children. The castle then came into the possession of the archbishop's eldest son, Dudley Loftus, knighted by Lord Deputy Fitzwilliam for his valour in the military operations in Ulster. Apparently, in an engagement near Beleek his horse was killed under him, after which Dudley killed twelve of the enemy with his own hands. At this time the castle was the residence of Sir Thomas Ridgeway, then treasurer of Ireland. Following Dudley's death in 1616 his eldest brother, Adam Loftus, took up residence at the castle. He had received a knighthood in 1610 from Sir Arthur Chichester, the planter of Ulster. On Shrove Monday 1632 his eldest son, Arthur, was married by Primate Henry Ussher in Rathfarnham Castle to the earl of Cork's daughter, Dorothy (aged 14), who had been born in Sir Walter Raleigh's house at Youghal. This was the beginning of a distinguished career for Adam Loftus, who soon became surveyor-general of Ireland and an official of the Court of Wards. He also acted as a keeper of the Great Seal during the absence of his cousin, Viscount Ely, and was made a member of the Privy Council, and later vice-treasurer of Ireland.

In 1724 the estate and castle of Rathfarnham were sold to William Conolly, speaker of the Irish House of Commons, for £62,000, though he never lived there. The castle was brought back into the Loftus family in 1767 by Nicholas Loftus, second earl of Ely, who remodelled the interior with fine stucco work. The essential plan of the original building remains unchanged, and consists of a rectangular central block with a spear-shaped tower at each of the corners. The lines of string-coursing are original, and reflect the internal floor levels. Missing are the typical musket-loops to defend the building at ground level. Shortly after 1767 Lord Ely had the battlements removed, and replaced the original small Gothic windows with the large Georgian windows that survive today. The semicircular extension at the east side was probably added about this time. In 1781 Austin Cooper was received at the castle and, suitably impressed, wrote: 'The Hall is but low, at the same time exquisitely elegant—on your right Hand are three Windows of Stained Glass done by Jervis, the Center one has his Lordship's Arms therein; all around are disposed a variety of Antique Busts, Inscriptions—Statues Urns &c. The Gallery is a beautiful room, at the far end is a curious Cabinet of Tortoise Shell & Brass containing some most extraordinary Work in Ivory.'

Shanganagh Castle

On private grounds in Shanganagh are the remains of a tower-house built around 1408 by Thomas Lawless. By 1447 the castle was occupied by Edmund Walsh. Only the west wall and the north-west angle of this small tower survive, with two massive fireplaces. It was described in the 1654 Civil Survey as a castle with a large thatched hall nearby (which was pulled down *c.* 1835), with two orchards, a garden, a grove of ash trees set for ornament, and a mill. A painting by Beranger *c.* 1760 shows the castle with crenellations at the top. The castle was severely damaged by fire in 1763.

Shankill

Marking the site of the archbishop's manor of Shankill is a tower-house, probably constructed during the first half of the fifteenth century by the Lawless family. In 1571 the castle was owned by Robert Barnewall, who later married a sister of his neighbour, Theobald Walsh of Carrickmines. The building is presently in a ruinous condition, and many later alterations have obliterated or masked earlier features. A fine vault extends above the ground floor, and at the north end is a large fireplace, on the right of which is a later brick oven. At the north-east angle is a tower containing a stone spiral staircase retaining many of the original narrow slit arrow-loops; the exterior of this tower has a pronounced batter. From this staircase the top floor can still be accessed. Most of the windows in the castle are eighteenth-century red brick enlargements of earlier windows. However, on the top floor in the west wall is a chamfered, mullioned, flat-lintelled granite window, probably an original feature. In the south wall is a defaced flat-hooded, three-light limestone window, probably inserted in the sixteenth century. Projecting in from the west wall are two opposing brick fireplaces, probably of eighteenth-century date,

Pl. 85—Shankill Castle.

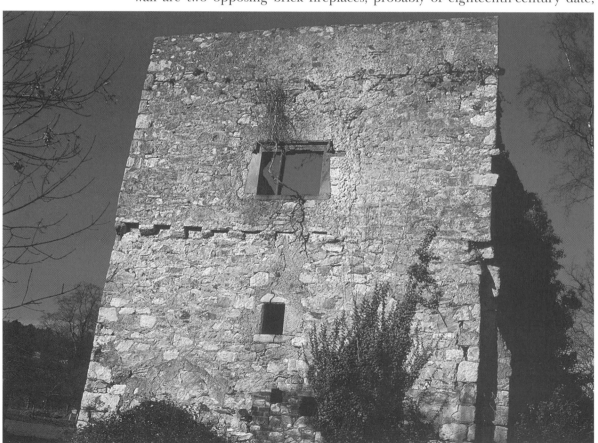

which indicate that the upper floor was divided into at least two rooms at this time.

In 1839 Lewis recorded that the castle was 'said to have been besieged by Cromwell, and near which have been frequently found human skeletons, and coins of the reigns of Chas. I and Jas. I. In a field belonging to Mr Hopper was discovered, in ploughing, a stone coffin containing human bones.' Perhaps these belonged to the cemetery of the old church of Shankill.

GLOSSARY

AMBRY: A small cupboard or niche used for storing vessels needed for the conduct of Mass.

ANTAE: The projection of the side walls beyond the gables of some early churches.

ARCHITRAVE: Plain or decorative moulding around a door or window opening.

BATTER: Receding upward slope of outer face of a wall.

BATTLEMENTS: A *parapet*, usually divided into short, solid merlons by regular openings or embrasures. Also called crenellation.

BAWN: Walled enclosure around a castle or tower-house, forming a defended yard.

BELLCOTE: Small stone structure housing a bell/bells on the roof of a church.

BOSS: Small domed projection.

BULLAUN: Hollowed-out basin in the surface of a stone, usually an unshaped boulder.

BURGAGES: Plots of land within a town with certain privileges granted to encourage settlers.

BUTTRESS: A mass of masonry projecting from or built against a wall to give additional strength.

CAPSTONE: A large stone or slab covering a megalithic tomb.

CHAMFER: The cut or bevelled edge of stonework.

CHANCEL: The eastern portion of a church, where the altar is situated. Often a separate compartment within the body of a church. The chancel arch is that which separates the *nave* from the chancel.

CHEVRON: A V-shaped ornament, producing a zigzag effect in succession.

CORBEL: Stone projecting from wall which supports floor beams, rafters or oversailing masonry.

DRESSED: Roughly faced and shaped stone.

DRYSTONE: Coursed or uncoursed masonry constructed without mortar.

EMBRASURE: The recesses for doorways and windows, or an opening in a parapet wall.

FALSE RELIEF: Sculpture whereby carvings appear to be in relief although they are actually no higher than the general surface.

FINIAL: A formal gable ornament of a church, or the gable-shaped capstone of a high cross.

GALLERY (megalithic tomb): An oblong or wedge-shaped compartment in which burials were deposited.

GARDEROBE: Medieval lavatory.

GLAZING BAR HOLES: Holes in the jambs of windows which supported the rods used to fix panes of glass in position.

HOOD-MOULDING: The projecting moulding placed around the top of a window, door or arch.

INHUMATION: Burial of unburnt human remains.

IN SITU: In the original position.

INTERLACE: Decorative system using intertwined strands in a complex pattern.

JAMB: The side of an arch, doorway or window.

JOISTS: The timbers supporting the floorboards.

KEEP: The principal tower of a castle.

KERB: Continuous line of stones or slabs surrounding the base of a cairn.

LINTEL: A horizontal stone covering a doorway.

LOOP: A small narrow light, of various forms, in a wall or at the angle of two walls, facilitating the release of projectiles such as arrows or gunshot.

LOZENGE MOTIFS: Diamond-shaped designs.

MACHICOLATION: A projecting *parapet* supported on *corbels* between which stones etc. could be dropped on assailants.

MORTICE: A hole made to receive and secure the end of another part, such as a *tenon*.

MULLION: The vertical post which divides a window into two or more lights.

NAVE: The main, western portion of a church, often a separate compartment from the *chancel*.

NICHE: A recess in a wall.

OGEE-HEADED: Arch over a window formed with reversed curves, giving an onion-shaped head.

ORTHOSTAT: Upright block of stone used to form the sides of chambers or passages in megalithic tombs.

PALISADE: A fence of timber stakes.

PARAPET: A low wall placed at the edge of a roof for protection, sometimes crenellated.

PLINTH: Foundation platform on which a building is constructed.

PUTLOG HOLE: An opening left in a wall for the insertion of scaffolding.

QUOINS: The stone blocks, set with their long and short sides alternating, forming the corners or angles of a building.

REBATE: A step-shaped channel or groove or a continuous rectangular notch or groove cut on an edge, so that a plank or door, etc., may be fitted into it.

SCARP: A sharp, steep slope created by cutting into a natural slope.

SHERDS: Fragments of pottery.

SOFFIT: The underside of an arch or lintel.

SPLAY: Sides of a window opening with obtuse or acute angles to the other wall faces.

SPRINGING: The starting-point of the curve of an arch or vault.

STOUP: A vessel to contain holy water, near a church doorway.

STRING-COURSE: A projecting horizontal band in a wall, often moulded.

TENON: A projecting piece of stone or wood, fitting into a socket or *mortice*.

TREFOIL: A three-lobed arch or a three-leafed motif.

VAULT: An arched structure of masonry usually forming a ceiling or roof.

WALL-WALK: A walkway positioned outside the roof and behind the parapet of a castle or church.

WICKER CENTRING: A temporary wicker framework used to support an arch or vault while it is under construction.

Bibliography

Aalen, F.H.A. and Whelan, K. (eds) 1992 *Dublin city and county: from prehistory to present.* Geography Publications, Dublin.

Anon. 1914 South County Dublin. *Journal of the Royal Society of Antiquaries of Ireland* **44**, 223–30.

Ball, F.E. 1897 Stillorgan Park and its history. *Journal of the Royal Society of Antiquaries of Ireland* **27**, 21–34.

Ball, F.E. 1900 Monkstown Castle and its history. *Journal of the Royal Society of Antiquaries of Ireland* **30**, 109–17.

Ball, F.E. 1901 The castle of Carrickmines and its history. *Journal of the Royal Society of Antiquaries of Ireland* **31**, 195–203.

Ball, F.E. 1902 *A history of the County Dublin, Part I.* Alex. Thom and Co., Dublin.

Ball, F.E. 1903 *A history of the County Dublin, Part II.* Alex. Thom and Co., Dublin.

Ball, F.E. 1905 *A history of the County Dublin, Part III.* Alex. Thom and Co., Dublin.

Barrow, G.L. 1979 *The round towers of Ireland.* Academy Press, Dublin.

Borlase, W.C. 1897 *The dolmens of Ireland, Vol. II.* Chapman and Hall, London.

Bourke, C. 1980 Early Irish hand-bells. *Journal of the Royal Society of Antiquaries of Ireland* **110**, 52–66.

Bradley, J. 1998 The medieval boroughs of County Dublin. In C. Manning (ed.), *Dublin and beyond the Pale. Studies in honour of Patrick Healy*, 129–44. Wordwell, Bray.

Breen, T.C. 1981 A pre-Norman grave-slab at Rathfarnham, County Dublin. *Journal of the Royal Society of Antiquaries of Ireland* **111**, 120–3.

Buckley, V. 1998 The excavation of a Bronze Age *fulacht fiadh* at Ballyremon Commons, Co. Wicklow. In C. Manning (ed.), *Dublin and beyond the Pale. Studies in honour of Patrick Healy*, 111–12. Wordwell, Bray.

Clare, L. 1998 *Victorian Bray—a town adapts to changing times.* Irish Academic Press, Dublin.

Corlett, C. 1998a The ritual landscape of the Great Sugar Loaf. *Wicklow Archaeology and History* **1**, 1–8.

Corlett, C. 1998b Recent finds from County Wicklow. *Wicklow Archaeology and History* **1**, 64–6.

Corlett, C. (ed.) (forthcoming) *The field notebooks of Liam Price.*

Corlett, C. and McGuinness, D. 1994 A grave-slab from Kiltiernan, south Dublin. *Journal of the Royal Society of Antiquaries of Ireland* **124**, 217–18.

County Wicklow Heritage Project 1993 *The emergence of Wicklow as a county, 1606–1845.* The County Wicklow Heritage Society.

Cromwell, T.K. 1820 *Excursions through Ireland. Province of Leinster.* London.

D'Alton, J. 1838 *The history of the county of Dublin.* Hodges and Smith, Dublin.

Daly, J.F. 1961 Curative wells in old Dublin. *Dublin Historical Record* **17** (1), 13–24.

Davies, K.M. 1986 The castle of Bray. *Journal of the Cualann Historical Society*, 22–5.

Davies, K.M. 1989a The cartographic record: Bray from maps. In J. O'Sullivan, T. Dunne and S. Cannon (eds), *The book of Bray*, 26–44. Blackrock Teachers' Centre, Blackrock.

Davies, K.M. 1989b The Meath estate. In J. O'Sullivan, T. Dunne and S. Cannon (eds), *The book of Bray*, 45–9. Blackrock Teachers' Centre, Blackrock.

Dolley, M. 1961 The 'lost' hoard of tenth-century Anglo-Saxon silver coins from Dalkey. *Journal of the Royal Society of Antiquaries of Ireland* **91**, 1–18.

Doran, A.L. 1985 *Bray and environs* (1st edn 1905). Kestral Books, Bray.

Eogan, G. 1968–9 'Lock-rings' of the Late Bronze Age. *Proceedings of the Royal Irish Academy* **67C**, 93–148.

Eogan, G. 1983 *Hoards of the Irish Later Bronze Age*. University College, Dublin.

Eogan, G. 1994 *The accomplished art*. Oxbow Monograph 42. Oxbow Books, Oxford.

Etchingham, C. 1994 Evidence of Scandinavian settlement in Wicklow. In K. Hannigan and W. Nolan (eds), *Wicklow: history and landscape*, 113–38. Geography Publications, Dublin.

Fanning, T. 1974 A wedge tomb at Laughanstown, Co. Dublin. *Journal of the Royal Society of Antiquaries of Ireland* **104**, 151.

Fitzgerald, W. 1909–11 The manor and castle of Powerscourt, Co. Wicklow, in the sixteenth century, formerly a possession of the earls of Kildare. *Journal of the Kildare Archaeological Society* **6**, 127–39.

Flynn, A. 1986 *History of Bray*. The Mercier Press, Bray.

Goodbody, R. 1993a Pale ditch in south County Dublin. *Archaeology Ireland* **7** (3), 24–5.

Goodbody, R. 1993b *On the borders of the Pale. A history of the Kilgobbin, Stepaside and Sandyford area*. Pale Publishing, Bray.

Grogan, E. and Hillery, T. 1993 *A guide to the archaeology of County Wicklow*. Wicklow County Tourism, Wicklow.

Grogan, E. and Kilfeather, A. 1997 *Archaeological Inventory of County Wicklow*. Stationery Office, Dublin.

Grose, F. 1791–5 *The antiquities of Ireland*. M. Hooper, London.

Hannigan, K. and Nolan, W. (eds) 1994 *Wicklow: history and landscape*. Geography Publications, Dublin.

Harbison, P. 1969 *The daggers and the halberds of the Early Bronze Age in Ireland*. C.H. Beck'sche Verlagsbuchhandlung, München.

Harbison, P. 1991 *Beranger's views of Ireland*. Royal Irish Academy, Dublin.

Harbison, P. 1998 *Beranger's antique buildings of Ireland*. Four Courts Press, in association with the National Library of Ireland, Dublin.

Hoare, P.G. 1975 The pattern of glaciation in County Dublin. *Proceedings of the Royal Irish Academy* **75B**, 207–24.

Joyce, W. St J. 1912 *The neighbourhood of Dublin*. M.H. Gill and Son, Dublin.

Kavanagh, R.M. 1973 Encrusted Urns in Ireland. *Proceedings of the Royal Irish*

Academy **73C**, 507–617.

Kavanagh, R.M. 1976 Collared and Cordoned Urns in Ireland. *Proceedings of the Royal Irish Academy* **76C**, 293–403.

Kavanagh, R.M. 1977 Pygmy cups in Ireland. *Journal of the Royal Society of Antiquaries of Ireland* **107**, 61–95.

Kerrigan, P.M. 1995 *Castles and fortifications in Ireland, 1485–1945.* The Collins Press, Cork.

Kilbride-Jones, H.E. 1939 Early Christian cemetery at Kilbride, near Bray, Co. Wicklow. *Journal of the Royal Society of Antiquaries of Ireland* **69**, 173–6.

Kilbride-Jones, H.E. 1954 The excavation of an unrecorded megalithic tomb on Kilmashoge Mountain, Co. Dublin. *Proceedings of the Royal Irish Academy* **56C**, 461–79.

Le Fanu, T.P. 1893 The Royal Forest of Glencree. *Journal of the Royal Society of Antiquaries of Ireland* **23**, 268–80.

Lewis, S. 1837 *A topographical dictionary of Ireland* (2 vols). Lewis and Co., London.

Liversage, D. 1968 Excavations at Dalkey Island 1956–1959. *Proceedings of the Royal Irish Academy* **66C**, 53–233.

Mac Cóil, L. 1977 *The book of Blackrock.* Carraig Books, Blackrock.

McDix, C. 1897 The lesser castles of the Co. Dublin: Puck's Castle. *The Irish Builder* (1 July), 129.

Mac Mahon, T. 1987 Rathfarnham Castle. *Dublin Historical Record* **41** (1), 21–3.

Manning, C. (ed.) 1998 *Dublin and beyond the Pale. Studies in honour of Patrick Healy.* Wordwell, Bray.

Martin, C.P., Price, L. and Mitchell, G.F. 1935–7 On two short cist interments found at Ballybrew, Co. Wicklow. *Proceedings of the Royal Irish Academy* **43C**, 255–70.

Mason, A. 1983 Cross-inscribed slab in Archbold's Castle, Dalkey, County Dublin. *Journal of the Royal Society of Antiquaries of Ireland* **113**, 143–4.

Mills, J. 1894 Norman settlement in Leinster: the Cantreds, near Dublin. *Journal of the Royal Society of Antiquaries of Ireland* **24**, 160–75.

Mount, C. and Hartnett, P.J. 1993 Early Bronze Age cemetery at Edmondstown, County Dublin. *Proceedings of the Royal Irish Academy* **93C**, 2–79.

Mount, C. and Keeley, V. 1990 An early medieval strap-tag from Balally, County Dublin. *Journal of the Royal Society of Antiquaries of Ireland* **120**, 120–5.

Nairn, R. and Crowley, M. 1998 *Wild Wicklow—nature in the Garden of Ireland.* Town House, Dublin.

Neary, P. 1992 A saddle quern or grinding stone from Rathdown Lower, Co. Wicklow. *Trowel* **3**, 9–11.

Nolan, K. 1939 The ancient church and parish of Kiltiernan, Co. Dublin. *Dublin Historical Record* **2** (1), 38–40.

O'Brien, E. 1988 Churches of south-east Dublin, seventh to twelfth century. In G. MacNiocaill and P.F. Wallace (eds), *Keimelia: studies in medieval archaeology and history in memory of Tom Delany*, 504–24. Galway University Press.

O'Brien, E. 1989 Excavations at Dundrum Castle, Dundrum, Co. Dublin. *Archaeology Ireland* **3** (4), 136–7.

O'Donovan, E. 1993 Full doorstones in portal tombs, precluding successive burials. *Trowel* **4**, 12–18.

O'Flanagan, M. 1927 Letters relating to the antiquities of the County of Dublin containing information collected during the progress of the Ordnance Survey in 1839. Unpublished typescript, Bray.

O'Flanagan, M. 1928 Letters relating to the antiquities of the County of Wicklow containing information collected during the progress of the Ordnance Survey in 1838. Unpublished typescript, Bray.

Ó hÉailidhe, P. 1957 The Rathdown slabs. *Journal of the Royal Society of Antiquaries of Ireland* **87**, 75–88.

Ó hÉailidhe, P. 1958 Fassaroe and associated crosses. *Journal of the Royal Society of Antiquaries of Ireland* **88**, 101–10.

Ó hÉailidhe, P. 1959 Some unpublished antiquities of the Early Christian period in the Dublin area. *Journal of the Royal Society of Antiquaries of Ireland* **89**, 205–7.

Ó hÉailidhe, P. 1973 Early Christian grave slabs in the Dublin region. *Journal of the Royal Society of Antiquaries of Ireland* **103**, 51–64.

Ó hÉailidhe, P. 1982 Three unrecorded early grave-slabs in County Dublin. *Journal of the Royal Society of Antiquaries of Ireland* **112**, 139–41.

Ó hÉailidhe, P. 1984 Decorated stones at Kilgobbin, County Dublin. *Journal of the Royal Society of Antiquaries of Ireland* **114**, 142–4.

Ó hÉailidhe, P. 1987 The cross base at Oldcourt, near Bray, Co. Wicklow. In E. Rynne (ed.), *Figures from the past: studies on figurative art in Christian Ireland in honour of Helen M. Roe*, 98–110. Glendale Press, Dublin.

Ó hÉailidhe, P. and Prendergast, E. 1977 Two unrecorded graveslabs in County Dublin. *Journal of the Royal Society of Antiquaries of Ireland* **107**, 139–42.

Ó h-Eochaidhe, M. 1957 Portal dolmen at Kiltiernan, Co. Dublin. *Proceedings of the Prehistoric Society* **23**, 221.

O'Keefe, T. 1992 Medieval frontiers and fortification: the Pale and its evolution. In F.H.A. Aalen and K. Whelan (eds), *Dublin city and county: from prehistory to present*, 57–77. Geography Publications, Dublin.

O'Neill, H. 1852–3 The rock monuments of the county of Dublin. *Journal of the Royal Society of Antiquaries of Ireland* **2**, 40–6.

Ó Nualláin, S. 1983 Irish portal tombs: topography, siting and distribution. *Journal of the Royal Society of Antiquaries of Ireland* **113**, 75–105.

O'Reilly, P.J. 1900 Tully, Rathmichael, Killiney and other places in south County Dublin. *Journal of the Royal Society of Antiquaries of Ireland* **30**, 181–92.

O'Reilly, P.J. 1901 The Christian sepulchral leacs and freestanding crosses of the Dublin half-barony of Rathdown. *Journal of the Royal Society of Antiquaries of Ireland* **31**, 134–61, 246–58, 385–404.

O'Reilly, P.J. 1902–4 Notes on the orientations and certain architectural details of the old churches of Dalkey town and Dalkey Island. *Proceedings of the Royal*

Irish Academy **24**, 195–226.

O'Reilly, P.J. 1904–5 Notes on the architectural details and orientations of the old churches of Kill-of-the-Grange, Killiney, and St Nessan, Ireland's Eye. *Proceedings of the Royal Irish Academy* **25**, 107–16.

Ó Ríordáin, B. and Waddell, J. 1993 *The funerary bowls and vases of the Irish Bronze Age*. Galway University Press.

Ó Ríordáin, S.P. 1947 Miscellaneous discoveries in the Dublin neighbourhood. *Journal of the Royal Society of Antiquaries of Ireland* **77**, 84–8.

Ó Ríordáin, S.P. and de Valéra, R. 1952 Excavation of a megalithic tomb at Ballyedmonduff, Co. Dublin. *Proceedings of the Royal Irish Academy* **55C**, 61–81.

O'Sullivan, J., Dunne, T. and Cannon, S. (eds) 1989 *The book of Bray*. Blackrock Teachers' Centre, Blackrock.

Pearson, P. 1998 *Between the mountains and the sea, Dun Laoghaire–Rathdown County*. The O'Brien Press, Dublin.

Price, L. 1930 Kilcrony Church. *Journal of the Royal Society of Antiquaries of Ireland* **60**, 179–81.

Price, L. 1934 The Ages of Stone and Bronze in County Wicklow. *Proceedings of the Royal Irish Academy* **42C**, 31–64.

Price, L. 1935 Cremated burial found near Enniskerry, Co. Wicklow. *Journal of the Royal Society of Antiquaries of Ireland* **65**, 325–6.

Price, L. 1938a Cist burial at Calary Lower, Kilmacanogue, Co. Wicklow. *Journal of the Royal Society of Antiquaries of Ireland* **68**, 157–9.

Price, L. 1938b Find of flat copper axes at Monastery, Co. Wicklow. *Journal of the Royal Society of Antiquaries of Ireland* **68**, 305–6.

Price, L. 1939 Find of flat copper axes at Monastery, Co. Wicklow. *Journal of the Royal Society of Antiquaries of Ireland* **69**, 50.

Price, L. 1940 The antiquities and place names of south Dublin. *Dublin Historical Record* **2** (4), 121–33.

Price, L. 1942 *An eighteenth century antiquary. The sketches, notes and diaries of Austin Cooper (1759–1830)*. Falconer, Dublin.

Price, L. 1953 Powerscourt and the territory of Fercullen. *Journal of the Royal Society of Antiquaries of Ireland* **83**, 117, 132.

Price, L. 1954 The grant to Walter de Ridelesford of Brien and the lands of the Sons of Turchill. *Journal of the Royal Society of Antiquaries of Ireland* **84**, 72–7.

Price, L. 1957 *Place names of County Wicklow, V. Barony of Rathdown*. Dublin Institute for Advanced Studies.

Price, L. 1959 Sculptured cross-base at Oldcourt, near Bray, Co. Wicklow. *Journal of the Royal Society of Antiquaries of Ireland* **89**, 97.

Saltzer, M. 1993 *Castles and stronghouses of Ireland*. Folly Publications, Worcs.

Scantlebury, C. 1960 A tale of two islands (Dalkey Island and Inis Pádraig). *Dublin Historical Record* **15**, 122–8.

Scantlebury, S.J. 1951 Rathfarnham Castle. *Dublin Historical Record* **12** (1), 20–30.

Scott, G.D. 1913 *The stones of Bray.* Hodges Figgis and Co., Dublin.

Simington, R. (ed.) 1945 *The Civil Survey A.D. 1654–1556, vii, County of Dublin.* The Stationery Office, Dublin.

Simpson, L. 1994 Anglo-Norman settlement in Uí Briúin Cualann. In K. Hannigan and W. Nolan (eds), *Wicklow: history and landscape,* 191–236. Geography Publications, Dublin.

Smith, C.V. 1995 An unpublished medieval deed from Dalkey, County Dublin. *Journal of the Royal Society of Antiquaries of Ireland* **125**, 46–50.

Smith, C.V. 1996 *Dalkey, society and economy in a small medieval Irish town.* Maynooth Studies in Local History No. 9. Irish Academic Press, Dublin.

Stokes, D.D. 1890–1 Killegar church. *Journal of the Royal Society of Antiquaries of Ireland* **21**, 443–9.

Stout, G. 1994 Wicklow's prehistoric landscape. In K. Hannigan and W. Nolan (eds), *Wicklow: history and landscape,* 1–40. Geography Publications, Dublin.

Stout, G. and Stout, M. 1992 Patterns in the past: Dublin 5000 BC–1000 AD. In F.H.A. Aalen and K. Whelan (eds), *Dublin city and county: from prehistory to present,* 5–14. Geography Publications, Dublin.

Swan, L. 1998 Lehaunstown Park, Co. Dublin: a forgotten tower house. In C. Manning (ed.), *Dublin and beyond the Pale. Studies in honour of Patrick Healy,* 163–8. Wordwell, Bray.

Turner, K. 1983 *If you seek monuments, a guide to the antiquities of the Barony of Rathdown.* Rathmichael Historical Society, Dublin.

Waddell, J. 1990 *The Bronze Age burials of Ireland.* Galway University Press.

Wakeman, W.F. 1890–1 Primitive churches in County Dublin. *Journal of the Royal Society of Antiquaries of Ireland* **21**, 697–702.

Wakeman, W.F. 1892 Ante-Norman churches in the county of Dublin. *Journal of the Royal Society of Antiquaries of Ireland* **22**, 101–6.

Wakeman, W.F. 1896 A descriptive sketch of places visited: Dalkey, etc. *Journal of the Royal Society of Antiquaries of Ireland* **26**, 403–18.

Wakeman, W.F. 1889–91 On the *bullán*, or rock-basin, as found in Ireland: with special reference to two inscribed examples. *Proceedings of the Royal Irish Academy* **17**, 257–64.

Warren, W.P. 1993 *Wicklow in the Ice Age—an introduction and guide to the glacial geology of the Wicklow district.* Department of Transport, Energy and Communications.

Westropp, T.J. 1913 Earthwork near Curtlestown, Co. Wicklow. *Journal of the Royal Society of Antiquaries of Ireland* **43**, 185–6.